THE
LONG-RUN
AVAILABILITY
OF
PHOSPHORUS

THE LONG-RUN AVAILABILITY OF PHOSPHORUS

A Case Study in Mineral Resource Analysis

Frederick J. Wells

Published for Resources for the Future, Inc.
By The Johns Hopkins University Press
Baltimore and London

Resources for the Future is a nonprofit corporation for research and education
in the development, conservation, and use of natural resources and the improve-
ment of the quality of the environment. It was established in 1952 with the coop-
eration of the Ford Foundation. Part of the work of Resources for the Future is
carried out by its resident staff; part is supported by grants to universities and
other non-profit organizations. Unless otherwise stated, interpretations and conclusions in RFF publications are those of the authors; the organization takes
responsibility for the selection of significant subjects for study, the competence of
the researchers, and their freedom of inquiry.

The figure for this book was drawn by Frank and Clare Ford. The book was
edited by John R. Tron and Jo Hinkel.

RFF editors: Herbert C. Morton, Joan R. Tron, Ruth B. Haas, Jo Hinkel

Contents

Foreword   ix

Acknowledgments   xi

Introduction   xiii

1   Reserves, Exhaustion Periods, and Costs   1
Estimates of "Usable" Supply   1
Crustal Phosphorus Supplies and Mining Costs   5
Summary of Exhaustion Period and Cost Estimates   10
Possible Additional Deposits and Future Costs   15

2   Projection Formulas for Fertilizer Consumption   25
The 2.7 Power Rule   25
The Modified FAO Fertilizer Prediction Formula   27
Revised FAO Formula Fertilizer Predictions   30

3   A Fertilizer Usage Function Based On
Physical Considerations   36
Multiple-Crop Experiments   36
De Wit's Theoretical Agricultural Output Limits   38
Ultimate Lower Limits of Per Capita Phosphorus
Consumption   41

4   Conservation and Recycling   46
Conservation Measures and Solutions   46
Recycling   53

5   Summary and Concluding Observations   60
Deposits   60
Phosphorus Fertilizer Consumption Estimates   62

Summary of Alternative Calculations   65
Results and Their Implications   68

Appendix A: Exhaustion Period Calculations and
Supplementary Tables   71

Appendix B: The 2.7 Power Equation for Estimating Fertilizer
Use Levels   88

Appendix C: Individual Country Comparisons   97

Appendix D: Erosion Control and Soil Fixation   107

Selected Bibliography   114

Index   119

TABLES

TABLE 1. Exhaustion Periods and Per Capita Costs for Phosphorus Derived from the 2.7 Rule   11

TABLE 2. Exhaustion Periods and Per Capita Costs for Phosphorus Derived from the Modified FAO Formula   32

TABLE 3. Comparisons of the Annual Production Rates Predicted by the 2.7 Rule and the Modified FAO Formula   33

TABLE 4. Exhaustion Times and Per Capita Costs Under Various Alternative Phosphorus Fertilizer Consumption Assumptions (for a Constant-Size World Population of 20 Billion)   66

TABLE A-1. Exhaustion Times and Per Capita Costs Under Various Alternative Phosphorus Fertilizer Consumption Assumptions (for a Constant-Size World Population of 12 Billion)   78

TABLE A-2. Exhaustion Times and Per Capita Costs Under Various Alternative Phosphorus Fertilizer Consumption Assumptions (for a Constant-Size World Population of 50 Billion)   80

TABLE A-3. Exhaustion Times and Per Capita Costs Under Various Alternative Phosphorus Fertilizer Consumption Assumptions (for a Constant-Size World Population of 100 Billion)   82

TABLE B-1. Actual and Predicted Fertilizer Use Growth Rates   92

TABLE C-1. Comparisons of the Phosphorus (P) Fertilizer Predictions from the 2.7 Rule and the FAO Equation with Individual Country Data   98

FIGURE

FIGURE 1. Projections of Phosphorus Consumption as a Function of Population and Food Production   26

Foreword

I am sure that many of those who, like myself, have been involved in the unending argument over adequacy of mineral (and other) resources to sustain specified levels of growth must often wonder whether there is not a better way of throwing light on the matter. The comparison of projected consumption levels, cumulated for three decades or half a century, with an estimate of materials in the ground deemed to be more or less economically recoverable, is an enterprise that can never be played to a conclusion. The uncertainties of the estimates aside, an optimistic finding can always be shaken by lengthening the projection period by a decade or two. If the world looks adequately "supplied" through the year 2000, then how about 2020? If through 2020, then how about 2050? Sooner or later the approach prejudices the outcome. As we try to perceive matters at a farther horizon we soon realize that even the rough dimensions of the relevant parameters become too dim to provide guidance.

Yet, the drive and, indeed, the sheer curiosity to ascertain in some useful form the shape of the future leave one dissatisfied with just giving up. The study prepared by Fred Wells suggests a way: go to the bitter end first and try to estimate the cost consequences of exhausting a given resource in its concentrated occurrences. Suppose we had to win phosphates from common rock. What would it cost? What would these costs do to agriculture? Would the cost be astronomical? Or just very high? In any event, are there obvious reductions to be assumed in such costs, or in other words, how bad does the "worst case" need to be made to be realistic?

Perhaps the specific findings are not as important, in this first attempt, as the way of getting at them. If this is a means of avoiding the tedious adequacy debate, let's do more of it, especially if the tour de force of a "worst case" exercise can then be brought closer to reality by introducing modifiers. Some of that too is in Wells' study. In any event, the project offers both a useful approach to the adequacy problem and, in the specific instance, an answer to suggestions made a few years ago that mankind was facing a phosphateless world within three or four generations. Indeed, it was this forecast that triggered the study, but its bearing soon went beyond.

In the process the author's research had to range far and wide, from crop response and nutrition problems to geology and engineering questions. Dogged persistence was paired happily with his multidisciplinary background, and the mix was aided by generous assistance from outside experts and reviewers. That we like the outcome is attested by its publication as an RFF product.

Hans H. Landsberg
Director, Division of Energy
and Resource Commodities

March 1975

Acknowledgments

My interest in doing this research was stimulated by, and stemmed from, some initial estimates made by Hal Goeller of Oak Ridge National Laboratory. His helpful comments at the early stages of the work are appreciated. Hans Landsberg of Resources for the Future also guided and encouraged me throughout the study and directed me to numerous other people for advice and subsequent review.

I am indebted to the following for providing advice about various aspects of the research: Charles Gibbons and Cliff Orvedal of the U.S. Department of Agriculture, Vincent McKelvey and Richard Sheldon of the U.S. Geological Survey, and Gilbert Terman of TVA. Toby Page of RFF gave me much encouragement and many helpful hints, but, more particularly, without him I could not have run or interpreted the regressions described in Appendix B. Cliff Orvedal, who reviewed the draft manuscript as well, was very helpful in providing instruction and guidance concerning the agricultural aspects of the study.

I also thank T. C. Byerly and Carl Carlson of the USDA, Lyle T. Alexander and Charles E. Kellogg, both formerly with the USDA, Robert Kelly and James Sawyer of RFF, Dr. G. Donald Emigh of Monsanto Chemicals, Professor Preston Cloud of the University of California, Santa Barbara, and Lewis B. Nelson and John Douglas of TVA, all of whom reviewed part or all of the draft manuscript and supplied helpful comments. Professor Frederick Smith of Harvard University supplied a very detailed critique which proved invaluable in revising the manuscript.

Joan Tron with the assistance of Jo Hinkel edited the manuscript with great care. I am indebted to Kay Albaugh and Helen-Marie Streich who typed and retyped the manuscript several times and managed successfully to struggle through several oversized tables.

Introduction

The Institute of Ecology (TIE) suggested in a 1971 report that known reserves of phosphorus (a metallic element with the atomic symbol P) might be depleted in sixty to ninety years.[1] In a 1972 revision of this report, the run-out period for P is reported as 90 to 130 years.[2] Because of the vital importance of phosphorus fertilizer in crop production, the original TIE report received wide publicity. The fact that much of the force of this report was dependent on a single, faulty figure, which, when corrected, dispelled some of the concern over the ultimate exhaustion of phosphorus supplies, is now known to specialists, but has not been widely publicized. However, the prime purpose of this analysis is to examine the running-out problem for mineral resources, using the phosphorus problem as a case study. The limited substitutability of other resources for phosphorus makes it an ideal candidate for such a study, since substitution possibilities could unduly complicate the analysis.

Our analysis is focused on the underlying assumptions and estimates that are essential in making such depletion period calculations. These involve assumptions about supplies and future consumption levels. Supply estimates are often complicated by terminology and technology assumptions. Assuming current technology, mineral supplies are usually broken down into reserves and resources. Reserves refer to supplies which can be mined and refined at or near prevailing market prices. This normally means deposits with relatively high percentages of the mineral element of interest. However, the term *reserve* is based on cost, not ore grade. Thus, a high-grade deposit might not be considered as part of reserves if the cost of obtaining the mineral is too high—for example, the total deposit is too small, located deep underground, under the sea, or too far away from convenient transportation, etc. *Resources* refer to supplies which cannot be obtained at or near current market prices. The cutoff between reserves and resources is never very sharp and varies as the price of the mineral goes up and down. A single deposit may contain both reserves and resources: as the price of the mineral element goes up, a larger fraction is counted as part of reserves and, often, a larger percentage of the mineral is recovered from any given volume of the deposit.

There are other modifiers of the words "reserves" and "resources," reflecting the feasibility of economic recovery and the degree to which the deposits are known to exist. One suggested breakdown employs the terms *proved, probable, possible* (all three of which occur in identified deposits) and *undiscovered* to suggest decreasing degrees of certainty concerning reserves and resources.[3] Relative costs are suggested by the terms *recoverable, paramarginal* and *submarginal.* Recoverable minerals in identified deposits form reserves, and all others are resources in this particular classification format.

Out of this maze of terms, it is clear that there is significant uncertainty over the quantities and costs involved. The best-known, and most widely quoted, figure is that of reserves. The exhaustion estimates by the TIE group were based on the reserve figures for phosphorus. This is a common approach for estimating exhaustion periods, but can be very misleading if additional supplies can be obtained even at higher costs than the current ones. However, the TIE group did acknowledge the possibility of finding and using supplies not included in the reserve estimates. Although they made a mathematical error, thus invalidating their calculation of additional supplies, the TIE group did make the assumption that an ore must contain at least 8 percent P to be "potentially usable." Whether an 8 percent ore grade is the dividing line between "usable" and "nonusable" deposits of phosphorus is a question we will address later, but the important point is that limiting usable supplies of P in this manner involves assumptions about technology and costs, as does any calculation for the running-out period.

It is rarely true, even with the existing level of technology, that there is some ore grade cutoff level below which a mineral element cannot be obtained. Instead, there may or may not be a fairly sharp increase in the costs of extraction for lower-grade ores or ores of a different chemical nature. Even if there are no substitutes for the mineral, the increase in costs for using lower-grade ores under existing technology may not be an impossible burden to bear, depending upon the per capita consumption levels. No matter what cost levels are expected for various grades and types of ores, the problem of running out is really one of costs—at some point the cost burden is so great as to reduce the per capita standard of living by some unacceptable percentage, perhaps so much as to threaten the existence of life. It is obvious that running out is not what is involved since, except for a very small amount of material which leaves our planet, everything we use is still here, although possibly so widely dispersed in very dilute quantities that recycling would be prohibitively expensive. Thus, any running-out calculation involves some assumption (perhaps not explicit) about what is an unacceptable cost burden to extract the mineral element in question.

In addition, there is also some assumption about technology involved. For example, is a "potentially usable" ore of an 8 percent grade usable under existing or some future technology? Since it usually is very difficult to estimate the capabilities of future technologies, the assumption (again, perhaps implicitly) is made that existing technology or limited extensions of that technology are to be considered. Since, by and large, twentieth-century history supports the proposition that increasing scarcity of higher-grade minerals has been offset by advances in technology, the assumption of little technology growth may be far wide of the mark. This is especially true where the reserves are to be depleted in a period of fifty years or more—it seems quite likely that relevant advances in technology will occur and help offset mineral extraction costs predicated on current technology.[4]

Assumptions concerning future consumption levels are probably even more perplexing. The TIE analysis of demand is based on the population level. Since population growth roughly follows an exponential growth pattern, their projections of phosphorus use also involve exponential growth. Although it is standard practice to employ exponential consumption growth formulas in projecting future usage, this approach may be very misleading for long-run projections. There may be no reason to believe that per capita usage of any given mineral will continue to grow at some given percentage rate every year. In general, per capita usage will vary according to technical and economic factors. Substitution, recycling, conservation, and changes in technology all significantly may change the growth rate in usage over long periods of time. Per capita usage levels for phosphorus are considered in this light in our analysis. Since, even if per capita usage remains constant, an exponentially growing population will create an exponential growth pattern, it can be seen that assumptions about population growth rates and ultimate world population levels are also crucial to exhaustion period calculations.

Definition of Terms

Since much of the analysis is a comparison with the TIE report and others, it would be useful to define the terms used here.

Supply Definitions.   In describing various estimates of reserves and resources, I shall use the following terms and definitions:

1. *Economic*, or *current*, or *commercial grade* reserves or deposits. These are high-grade ores currently being mined, including ores with extraction and beneficiation costs at or very close to the current levels.
2. *Subeconomic deposits.* These are the same, with somewhat higher costs.
3. *Low-grade deposits.* Those with even higher costs and generally encompassing ores containing roughly between 1 and 5 percent P.
4. *Common rock deposits.* Those with about 0.1 percent P.

Low-grade deposits really are intended to cover all the ores with costs between subeconomic deposits and common rock deposits. As these definitions have been picked to correspond to various supply estimates, their meaning will become clearer in the next chapter.

It should be noted that these definitions depart from the terms discussed above. Usually *reserve* means what we have termed *current* or *economic* deposits, while subeconomic deposits, low-grade deposits, and common rock deposits would be called various grades of "resources." We avoid the term *resource* for these types of ores and instead use the word to mean all ore of any grade. Both the terms *reserves* and *resources* tend to be misleading by themselves since they suggest that any reserve or resource is "usable" at or near current cost levels. The costs of extraction and beneficiation can vary widely for various ore bodies, and these costs affect the estimates given in the various sources cited here. Therefore, the terms *economic, subeconomic, low-grade,* and *common rock* have been employed to call attention to this.

The TIE conclusions that we would run out of P in about a century were based on what we have defined as economic or current deposits. They also provide an upper bound estimate of "potentially usable" supplies (ores with at least 8 percent P), and this estimate probably comes close to including what we have called economic deposits and subeconomic deposits. However, some ores with less than 8 percent P are part of current deposits and are now being mined; other ores with at least 8 percent P would not be considered as either economic or subeconomic to mine, beneficiate, and market because of such factors as the small size of the ore deposit, the distance to markets, the depth underground or other locational barriers, the difficulties of separating and upgrading the P in the ore, and other economic and technical factors. The category of ores with at least 8 percent P content thus cuts across our categories but perhaps corresponds roughly to the total of economic and subeconomic deposits.

Phosphorus Types and Uses.   This study, as well as the TIE report, concentrates its attention on inorganic, rather than organic P, and on its major use; that is, as commercial fertilizer.

There is no substitute for phosphorus as a plant food element, but organic sources such as animal manures and plant wastes could support a population of about 1 or 2 billion, according to the TIE study. While it is assumed that total world fertilizer usage of inorganic phosphorus greatly exceeds that of organic P, and commercial (inorganic) P fertilizer has largely displaced organic sources in the developed countries, the exact figures are not available. However, we do know that about 75 percent of the inorganic P in the United States (and a higher percentage in other countries) is used for fertilizer.[5] The other uses of inorganic P, such as in soaps, metal plating, and steel alloys, are neither large in amount nor essential, since there are possible substitutes for it in these uses.[6]

While there will be some discussion of organic phosphorus in the section devoted to recycling of organic plant and animal materials, the availability of inorganic phosphorus for commercial fertilizers is our primary concern.

When used as fertilizer, elemental phosphorus is combined with other elements and compounds. However, to simplify matters, all figures have been converted to the element basis here. In fact, however, only 10 or 20 percent of the weight of commercial phosphate fertilizer may be phosphorus.

Units of Measure. Figures have been expressed primarily in metric terms. The important equivalencies are: 1 kilogram (kg.) equals 2.2046 pounds; 1,000 kg. is 1 metric ton, which equals 1.1 U.S. (short) ton; 10,000 square meters (m^2) is 1 hectare (ha.), which equals 2.47 acres; 1,000,000 m^2 is 1 square kilometer (km.^{2}), which equals 0.3861 square miles.

The terms *million* (1,000,000 or 10^6), *billion* (1,000 million or 10^9), and *trillion* (1,000 billion or 10^{12}) are used throughout.

Price Levels and Base Year Dates. Most data for fertilizer usage, population levels, and prices are based on the 1968–70 period. More recent data are available in most cases, but, because of the very long-run point of view taken here, use of later data would not change our results in any significant way. Use of the 1968–70 data allows direct comparison with the TIE results, which also employ these data. In addition, price and wage controls, rapid inflation, the oil embargo, unanticipated increases in world demands for raw materials, and other factors make later figures highly unreliable guides for long-run prediction purposes.

Limitations of the Analysis

No position is taken in this study with respect to current environmental matters such as phosphorus mining wastes, flourine released to the atmosphere in processing phosphate rock, trace contaminants in phosphorus fertilizer, and the heavily debated topic of phosphate-induced eutrophication of water bodies. While some of the conservation measures advocated by the TIE panel may be justified on environmental grounds alone, others depend upon the scarcity argument, and it is the latter that are of concern since the additional expenditures implied may not be justified on scarcity grounds alone.[7] Judgments with respect to current environmental matters is left to others with competence in those fields.

Nor is any position taken regarding desirable population levels, despite the fact that calculations are included for world population levels up to 100 billion people. An upper limit of 100 billion population was selected as a number which would probably represent an extreme case. Indeed, a world population of 50 or 100 billion might not be sustainable for reasons other than phosphorus scarcity (e.g., environmental limits). Use of any given population level does not imply approval of that size population. To some, a long-run limit on world population of 1 or 2 billion might be very desirable but the merit of this stand is not argued here. The issue covered is whether or not (or more precisely, when and at what cost) we might be running out of phosphorus.

Study Outline

In Chapter 1 various estimates of phosphorus supplies and costs are presented. These include the TIE estimates, an estimate by Dr. G. D. Emigh, and an estimate of common rock supplies. A rough estimate of the costs of phosphorus from the last-mentioned source is described. Based on the TIE consumption formula, exhaustion periods and per capita costs are developed for several levels of population for each supply estimate.

Chapters 2 through 4 concentrate on the phosphorus consumption projection formulas. In Chapter 2 the 2.7 power rule used in the TIE study is contrasted with a projection equation developed by the Food and Agriculture Organization (FAO) of the United Nations. The exhaustion periods and per capita costs are recalculated with a modified form of the FAO equation in that chapter. An alternative phosphorus consumption equation based on physical plant requirements is derived in Chapter 3. Conservation and recycling of phosphorus are discussed in Chapter 4. In the concluding chapter, the main parts of the analysis are summarized. In particular, exhaustion periods and per capita costs for phosphorus are calculated with the various consumption projection equations for the various supply estimates. The implications of these results are then described.

Many of the details, especially mathematical matters, have been put into the appendices. Appendix A contains the details of the calculations of the exhaustion periods and per capita usage levels for the 2.7 power rule and the FAO equation. Additional summary tables similar to those in Chapter 5 are included in Appendix A as well. The underlying statistical analysis for the 2.7 power rule and a comparison of recent trends to the predictions of that rule are considered in Appendix B. In Appendix C data for individual countries are utilized to compare the phosphorus fertilizer consumption projections of the 2.7 power rule and the FAO equation. Appendix D contains a discussion of erosion losses and soil fixation of phosphorus. These two topics are relevant to the derivation of the phosphorus fertilizer consumption rule in Chapter 3.

Notes

[1] The Institute of Ecology, *Man in the Living Environment*, Report of the 1971 Workshop on Global Ecological Problems (Chicago: The Institute of Ecology, 1971), p. 55.

[2] The Institute of Ecology, *Man in the Living Environment*, revised edition (Madison: University of Wisconsin Press, 1972), p. 55. Further references to these books are indicated as the TIE report. So far as phosphorus is concerned, the material and paging in the two editions are the same except that the reserve figures and run-out times are larger in the 1972 edition.

[3] V. E. McKelvey, "Mineral Resource Estimates and Public Policy," in Donald A. Probst and Walden P. Pratt, eds., *United States Mineral Resources*, Geological Survey Professional Paper 820 (Washington, D.C.: Government Printing Office, 1973), pp. 9–19.

[4] Nevertheless, we also assume little or no technological progress in our analysis because of the difficulty in predicting what impact that would have.

[5] Richard W. Lewis, "Phosphorus," in U.S. Bureau of Mines, *Mineral Facts and Problems* (Washington, D.C.: Government Printing Office, 1970), p. 1150.

[6] Ibid., pp. 1146–1147.

[7] It should be noted that none of the TIE recommended conservation measures, including those depending on scarcity, have been directly analyzed here. Thus, even if our conclusions on scarcity are accepted, recommendations to conserve phosphorus mine tailings and to conserve phosphorus in usage may still be valid. To come to conclusions on these various specific TIE recommendations would require analysis of their specific costs and benefits, and this we have not done. Nevertheless, it should be noted that depletion allowances (14 percent for phosphorus) to offset federal income taxes are usually regarded as undesirable by economists.

1

Reserves, Exhaustion Periods, and Costs

Estimates of "Usable" Supply

The Institute of Ecology Estimates.   To estimate future consumption
of inorganic commercial fertilizer containing phosphorus, the TIE
panel relied on an empirically derived finding that a 2.7 percent increase in fertilizer (and other inputs) is required to yield a 1 percent
increase in crop output. In other words, if crop output keeps pace with
population growth, fertilizer use must increase 2.7 times faster than
the population.[1]

In the first edition of the TIE report, the following calculation based
on this 2.7 rule is provided. Given a 1968 world fertilizer consumption
of 7.6 million metric tons of P per year and known (economic) deposits, adjusted for mining and refinery losses, of 3.14 billion metric
tons of P,[2] application of the 2.7 rule to a world population growing
at 1.9 percent per year leads to the calculated conclusion that exhaustion occurs in sixty years, when the population has reached 11 billion.[3]

In the revised edition of the TIE report the calculation base is
changed from 1968 fertilizer usage (7.6 million tons of P per year) to
total production (11.3 million tons per year) for all uses including industrial and commercial applications. On the one hand, this is a more
realistic base since fertilizer applications ignore losses and under-
reporting from the production point of phosphate rock to the farmers'

1

fields. On the other hand, the utilization of total production assumes that nonfertilizer uses of P also increase 2.7 percent per 1 percent increase in population—and it is likely that this overestimates such uses. Because it is used in the revised TIE study and because it provides a "conservative" upper bound (i.e., it leads to overestimates of P consumption), the figure of 11.3 million tons per year is employed as the base-year usage in all remaining calculations here.

In the original 1971 edition of the TIE report, the economic deposits were listed as 3.14 billion tons of P. In the revised 1972 edition, the estimate of these economic deposits is increased to about 20 billion tons of P, in keeping with the U.S. Bureau of Mines estimate of "known and potential reserves."[4] While this estimate includes deposits which could be counted as subeconomic, it seems reasonable to term this as an estimate of economic or current commercial grade deposits. Even if this is not accurate, we shall for convenience label these 20 billion tons as economic deposits.

Given a 1968 production of 11.3 million tons of P per year and a world population of 3.6 billion growing at 1.9 percent per year, the 20 billion tons is exhausted in approximately ninety years according to the 2.7 rule.[5] The world population at that point would be approximately 20 billion.

While admitting that additional supplies and lower-grade deposits might extend the run-out date, the TIE group buttressed its argument with the following estimate of the maximum amount of what they believed to be "potentially usable" supplies—both known and still undiscovered.

The total phosphorus supply, however, is not limitless. An upper boundary can be set by the accumulated effects of erosion and deposition on this planet over the last half billion years. The total amount of primary (igneous) rock eroded has mobilized an estimated 1,600,000 million tons of phosphorus. Sedimentary rocks account for the loss (at concentrations of less than 0.1 percent phosphorus) of about 1,000,000 million tons. Thus, about 600,000 million tons may exist in materials with higher concentrations. The great bulk of this is not likely to contain more than one or two percent phosphorus. If as much as five percent is sufficiently rich in phosphorus to be potentially usable (eight percent or more), then no more than 30,000 million tons of usable phosphorus exist on the planet. Supplies are limited.[6]

Thus, the TIE group agreed that current reserves were on the order of 20 billion tons but that at most only an additional 10 billion tons of usable phosphorus might be found. However, an error was uncovered that would increase each of the tonnage figures in the passage above by a factor of 1,000.[7] Therefore, based on this TIE calculation, the "potentially usable" ore contains 30 trillion tons of P rather than 30 billion tons.[8] A stable population of 20 billion people would run through 30 trillion tons of P in about 26,000 years, since annual use of P would be on the order of 1.16 billion tons.[9] For a (possibly infeasible) world population of 50 billion, annual consumption would be about 13.75 billion tons per year and the 30 trillion tons of "usable phosphorus" would last about 2,200 years. Thus, the future date for running out of phosphorus may be rather far off.

Emigh's Estimates.   G. Donald Emigh, an acknowledged authority on phosphate supplies and director of mining for the Monsanto Industrial Chemicals Company, takes issue with the TIE estimates as given in the original 1971 TIE report.[10] He argues that present commercial grade deposits, known and potential, contain about 20 billion tons of P—and in the revised TIE report this figure was adopted. With greater relevance to our purposes, Emigh convincingly shows that the known "usable" deposits of subeconomic phosphorus are much greater than the maximum amount of 30 billion tons of P indicated in the TIE report. (At the time of his writing the factor-of-1,000 error had not been discovered.) Emigh calculates very conservatively from specific known ore deposits that, above and beyond the 20 billion tons of economic reserves, there are at least 160 billion tons of unmined phosphorus in ores of lower grade,[11] which contain in the majority of cases 8 percent or more phosphorus—in contrast to commercial grade deposits which generally contain, after some beneficiation, about 12 percent P. Although he cannot give actual figures, he indicates that there are many additional deposits which could greatly expand this total quantity of subeconomic or near-economic unmined phosphorus, and even greater quantities of P in lower-grade deposits.

The dispute here between Emigh and the TIE panel is really over what is a usable ore. The TIE group states that the 20 billion tons "includes rock with a phosphorus content as low as 8%, which though not now economically useful, is expected to become so in the future"[12]; and also argues that the ore must contain at least 8 percent P to be potentially usable. Emigh points out[13]:

The authors [of the TIE report] seem confused over the meaning of 8 percent phosphorus in rock as being too low grade to be economically used today. One Western U.S. rock producer mines and uses substantial quantities of 8 percent P rock without beneficiation. It also appears probable the authors do not know that the average grade of the ore mined in Florida, the largest phosphate rock producing area in the world, is only 3 percent to 4.5 percent P.

The confusion here is probably compounded because of the terms *ore* and *rock*. Generally phosphate ore refers to naturally occurring phosphate which is too low grade to be converted directly into fertilizer in a fertilizer production plant. In contrast, and perhaps somewhat strangely to an outsider, phosphate rock refers to a higher-grade phosphorus product which can be used in a fertilizer plant (or can be used directly on crops). In some instances, as Emigh notes, the naturally occurring material is of high enough grade to be dug out of the ground and shipped to a fertilizer manufacturing plant directly, and in these cases the material is also referred to as phosphate rock. In contrast, most phosphate material is a lower-grade ore and subjected to simple beneficiation (washing and flotation) at or near the mine site in order to obtain a higher-grade rock, which is then shipped to a fertilizer plant. Thus, the 20-billion-ton Bureau of Mines estimate appearing in the revised TIE report has an average of about 12 percent P in the *beneficiated phosphate rock* while the phosphate *ore* contains only around 6 percent P.[14] Because of this unfamiliar trade terminology, the TIE panel may have confused the percentage P content of the ore in the ground with the percentage P content of the beneficiated ore.

Thus, a fair conclusion is that the 20 billion ton estimate refers to *known and potential* deposits which will largely be quite *economic*, or what Emigh calls commercial grade. In contrast, the 160 billion ton estimate of Emigh refers to *known* deposits of *subeconomic* grade ores—but still "usable" although at a somewhat higher cost (with current technology). The sharp dividing line between usable and nonusable ores drawn by the TIE panel does not exist in this case: with a given state of technology, the costs of extracting and beneficiating the ore into rock simply rise as ore grade declines and other factors (location, physical formation, etc.) become less favorable.

Based on Emigh's ore deposit estimates, it is possible to calculate exhaustion or run-out times with the 2.7 power rule. If the economic deposits of 20 billion tons are supplemented by the subeconomic deposits of 160 billion tons, the total is 180 billion tons of P. Because Emigh has already directly allowed for some losses in extracting the P, has not included certain deposits due to lack of information, and has conservatively calculated the deposits actually included, it is assumed that 180 billion tons is the amount of "usable" P which can be recovered after allowance for losses in mining and beneficiating the ore.[15]

For a population of 12 billion, with an estimated annual phosphorus usage of about 290 million metric tons, 180 billion tons would last over 600 years. Since it would take additional time to reach a population of 12 billion and, during that growth period, calculated consumption would be less than 290 million tons of phosphorus per year, the reserve would last slightly longer than 600 years. For a stable population of 20 billion persons and an estimated annual phosphorus consumption of about 1.16 billion tons, 180 billion tons would be consumed in about 150 years. Again, this would be extended somewhat because of a lower annual consumption rate for years when the population had not yet reached its stable level of 20 billion.

Crustal Phosphorus Supplies and Mining Costs

Deposit Size and Exhaustion Time Estimates. As Emigh has suggested, phosphorus might some day be extracted from ores now considered quite uneconomic. While data on these low-grade ores are not available (although they are discussed, to some extent, later in this study), it is possible to calculate the amount of P in one of the least promising, highest-cost, last resort sources—namely, common rock, which contains only about 0.1 percent P.[16] This 0.1 percent P content of common rock contrasts sharply with that of current commercial grade deposits, the P content of which probably averages about 12 percent; even the P content of the 160 billion tons of P in the subeconomic deposits identified by Emigh averages around 8 percent; the low-grade deposits, for which data do not exist, include all P in deposits above the common rock level but below the subeconomic grade level.

Although it is perhaps unlikely that common rock will ever be mined at all, let alone mined for phosphorus by itself, an examination of the possibility for doing so gives us the upper limits of availability of this source, as well as the upper limits involved in mining increasingly less economic deposits. The calculations below relating to common rock should be regarded in just this hypothetical upper limit manner rather than as a suggestion that we might use this source at some time. Even if common rock were to become a source of minerals, it is generally agreed that several minerals would be extracted rather than just one as we have postulated, since by-product mining would probably reduce unit (per ton) costs by a significant amount.

The average continental crustal abundance (called the clarke) of P is about 1,050 parts per million (0.105 percent).[17] The weight of the topmost mile of the 50 million square miles (130 million km.^{2}) of land on the continents (excluding Antarctica) is estimated, at 2.7 gm per cubic centimeter, to be 5.6×10^{17} metric tons. Thus, the topmost mile (1.6 km.) holds about 5.9×10^{14} metric tons of P. Obviously, not all this could be extracted, but on the other hand, current mining operations already extend down 2 miles (3.2 km.), so the amount that at least in principle might be extracted is of this order of magnitude. For a 20 billion population consuming 1,160 million tons of phosphorus per year, 5.9×10^{14} tons would last about 500,000 years.[18]

Mining and Beneficiating Costs. K. B. Brown, of Oak Ridge National Laboratory (ORNL), has estimated that extracting phosphorus, or more exactly the mineral-bearing phosphorus compounds, from Conway granites, a 0.1 percent P ore, would run about 200 times present costs.[19] H. E. Goeller, also of ORNL, comments that Brown has preliminarily estimated that "the cost of mining and beneficiating phosphate from average granite to a point suitable for chemical fertilizer manufacture would be in the range of $4000/ton of contained P_2O_5 (or $9000/ton of P), about 200 times the present [1972] cost of $20/ton of P_2O_5."[20]

Goeller describes the origin of this estimate in the following way: "K. B. Brown made quite good cost estimates on recovering thorium from Conway granites about 10 years ago. Recently A. M. Weinberg [director of the Oak Ridge Laboratory] asked him to guess what phosphates from this source might cost; his guess-timate was about 200 times present costs."[21] In this connection it is mentioned that by-product thorium and other minerals might also be extracted to reduce unit costs. Brown in his memo states, "Although drawing analogies can sometimes be treacherous, it does not seem unreasonable to use the information which we previously developed for recovering thorium and uranium from granites in guess-timating the cost for recovering phosphate from granites, [but] . . . these estimates, of course, are very much in the back-of-the-envelope category, [and] . . . some of the basic assumptions may be in error."

This estimate is based on the current state of the art—machines and processes which, although they do not all exist now, could be assembled from existing technology. Brown states in his memo:

It is assumed that 50 percent of the P_2O_5 could be recovered by flotation processing of granite that had been crushed to a point of mineral liberation. The assumption of flotation processes extends beyond experimental support since, to my knowledge, no one has attempted such processing. It is a fact, however, that fine grained phosphate minerals (apatite) are currently recovered from the fine, clay-like portions of the Florida phosphate beds by flotation processing.

In contrast, Emigh has expressed the opinion that the $10,000 per ton cost is far too high and his guess would be a "fraction" of this.[22]

A very crude check on this cost estimate is the cost of copper, which, in some cases, is mined from ore containing less than 0.5 percent copper.[23] The costs of refined electrolytic copper, at least 99.9 percent pure, vary widely over time but seem to have averaged under 50 cents per pound, or $1,000 per short ton. While the granite ore of phosphorus is less concentrated (0.1 percent P) than the copper ore (0.5 percent Cu), phosphorus is not refined to the level copper is. Despite very large differences in the beneficiating and refining of these two substances, the relative closeness of the estimated cost for phosphorus to the actual cost of copper is somewhat reassuring.

Environmental Mining Costs.   The $10,000 per metric ton estimate for phosphorus does not include the environmental costs of mining or of eutrophication from phosphate waste discharges. While the eutrophication problem from phosphate fertilizer is probably independent of the type of rock from which the phosphorus is taken, certainly the mining damages are not.[24] Current estimates for coal strip-mining reclamation run from $500 to $1,600 per acre ($1,200 to $4,000 per hectare) depending on the terrain and level of reclamation.[25] In certain unfavorable instances, even the highest reclamation expenditure of $1,600 per acre does not suffice to restore the land to its original condition. In Germany, where strip mining on flat areas for brown coal and extensive land rehabilitation has been practiced for many years, restoration of this flat land to full agricultural productivity costs between $3,000 and $4,500 per acre ($7,400 and $11,000 per hectare).[26] Costs for restoration to other uses such as lakes and forests are evidently somewhat lower.

Underground mining of P would also have its environmental costs. Subsidence and water drainage problems associated with underground coal mining indicate control costs of well under $1.00 per ton of coal but, again, some problems remain, especially in the case of surface subsidence.[27] Careful measures to control subsidence might become quite expensive. One solution is to mine only part of the ore to prevent surface settling. It is assumed in the calculations below that only half the ore is mined down to a level of two miles (3.2 km.). This maintains the resource base at the same level but reduces the subsidence problem to some extent. Nevertheless, a serious subsidence problem (or other environmental problems) might still persist.

It is also relevant to calculate the annual surface area under which mining would be needed to supply phosphorus. At a density of 2.7 gm per cubic centimeter, there are about 1.1×10^{10} (11 billion) metric tons of material in each cubic mile (2.7 billion tons per cubic kilometer). Mining two miles down, with 50 percent recovery of a 0.1 percent ore, provides 11 million metric tons of phosphorus under each square mile (430 thousand tons per square kilometer). For the calculated annual consumption of 1,160 million tons for a population of 20 billion people, the equivalent of about 100 square miles (270 km.²) would be mined out each year.[28] If one's time horizon is limited to 1,000 years, 100,000 square miles (270,000 km.²) are involved—an area of about 300 by 300 miles, about the size of New York and Pennsylvania combined—a considerable amount of land to be essentially stripped out and then replaced.

These large volumes and areas are also significant because, after crushing, the rock volume would increase 20–40 percent.[29] Disposal of this extra volume would perhaps necessitate very large tailings piles or dumping into the ocean. Problems with acid mine water would have to be controlled as well.

Assume, in the face of all these magnitudes, that an extra $1,000 per ton of P is provided for environmental mining control costs. Then, with 11 million tons recovered per square mile of surface, environmental mining expenditures would amount to 11 billion dollars per square mile, or $17 million per acre ($42 million per hectare). Although by present standards this is an immense amount, in view of the possible ecological risks and damages it still might not be adequate. Nevertheless, this figure will be used in the calculations, in the expectation that considerable improvements in the technology of ecological preservation would be achieved before (or if) resort to this source of P would become necessary.

Total and Per Capita Phosphorus Costs. Costs per metric ton of P, beneficiated but not transported or converted into fertilizer, would then total $11,000. This figure does not allow for the environmental damage that phosphate fertilizer runoff would bring about, but this topic will be touched on later. At $11,000 per ton of P, 20 billion people consuming 1,160 million tons per year would have an annual phosphate bill of $12.8 trillion ($12.8 \times 10^{12}$), or $640 per capita.[30] Even at current income levels this per capita cost would not present any insurmountable problem in the developed countries. It is in the developing world, where $640 is usually larger than total annual per capita income, that serious difficulties could arise. However, as such expensive sources of phosphate are not likely to be utilized for at least several centuries (if ever), it may be expected that most of the world would achieve at least U.S. income levels by then.[31]

Small increases in fertilizer costs now or in the immediate future are likely to be much more important to the less-developed countries than fairly large increases in the far future. However, as Emigh's data on phosphate rock supplies that can be mined at current costs indicate, the price of phosphate should not increase much for a very long time.[32]

Summary of Exhaustion Period and Cost Estimates

The TIE Estimates of Current Deposits.   Table 1 contains a summary of the calculations to this point. The first two lines are based on the original (1971) TIE study calculations with current, commercial grade deposits of 3.14 billion tons of P and a 7.6 million ton 1968 consumption of P. Line 1 provides an estimate of static reserves—413 years—since it is assumed that population does not increase above the 1968 level. For a current (1972) cost of $50 per metric ton of P, or 5 cents per kilogram, the current average worldwide annual per capita expenditure on P for fertilizer application is about 11 cents.[33] Clearly, the condition that population will remain at the current level will not hold. Thus, based on the original TIE estimate of the recoverable known reserve, a population growing at a constant rate of 1.9 percent per year would exhaust this reserve in sixty years (line 2 of Table 1).

All the remaining TIE entries are based on the revised (1972) TIE report. On lines 3 and 4, the 1968 production figure of 11.3 million tons is substituted for the 1968 consumption of 7.6 million tons and the economic deposit figure is increased from 3.14 billion tons to 20 billion tons. The static reserve is then increased to 1,750 years (line 3), and the exhaustion time for a population constantly growing at 1.9 percent per year is increased to eighty-eight years (line 4).

TABLE 1. Exhaustion Periods and Per Capita Costs for Phosphorus Derived from the 2.7 Rule

Source of deposit estimate[a] and case number	Average grade of ore (% P) (1)	Recoverable amounts of P (billion tons) (2)	Ultimate population (billions) (3)	Annual use of P at ultimate population level (million tons) (4)	Total years to exhaustion (5)	At ultimate population level (Col. 3)		
						Annual consumption of P per person (kg.) (Col. 4 ÷ Col. 3) (6)	Price of P ($/ton) (7)	Annual per capita cost ($/person) (Col. 6 × Col. 7 ÷ 1,000) (8)
Current and subeconomic deposits								
TIE original								
1	12.0	3.14	3.6[b]	7.6	413	2.1	50	0.11
2	12.0	3.14	11.3	169.0	60	14.9	50	0.75
TIE revised								
3	12.0	20	3.6[b]	11.3	1,750	3.1	50	0.16
4	12.0	20	19.2	1,040.0	88	54.0	50	2.70
5	12.0	20	12	292.0	113	24.3	50	1.22
Emigh								
6	8.0	180	12	292.0	660	24.3	(50)[c]	(1.22)[c]
7	8.0	180	20	1,160.0	226	57.9	(50)	(2.90)
8	8.0	180	43.2	9,250.0	131	214.0	(50)	(10.70)
Long-run and common rock deposits								
TIE revised								
9	8.0	30,000	12	292.0	103,000	24.3	(50)	(1.22)
10	8.0	30,000	20	1,160.0	26,000	57.0	(50)	(2.90)
11	8.0	30,000	50	13,700.0	2,300	275.0	(50)	(13.70)
12	8.0	30,000	100	89,300.0	491	893.0	(50)	(44.70)
Common rock								
13	0.1	590,000	12	292.0	2,020,000	24.3	11,000	267.00
14	0.1	590,000	20	1,160.0	509,000	57.9	11,000	637.00
15	0.1	590,000	50	13,700.0	43,000	275.0	11,000	3,020.00
16	0.1	590,000	100	89,300.0	6,760	893.0	11,000	9,830.00

Note: Tonnage figures in all tables refer to metric tons.

[a] In all but the first two lines, the 1968 base consumption of phosphorus is taken as the 1968 production figure of 11.3 million tons. The first two lines are based on a 1968 consumption of 7.6 million tons as in the original Institute of Ecology report.

[b] 1968 world population.

[c] The price and cost figures in parentheses are to be interpreted as lower bound estimates. See text for explanation.

In contrast to line 4, the population in line 5 is assumed to grow at 1.9 percent per year for sixty-three years when it reaches 12 billion and then to cease growing and remain at 12 billion thereafter. Such a pattern of population growth is not very likely but is just a simplified representation of what would be a more complicated growth pattern. In reality, if the population were to stabilize at 12 billion, the rate of population growth would slow down more gradually and would take longer to reach the equilibrium level (provided the maximum rate of growth did not exceed 1.9 percent per year). In this event the calculations provide an overestimate of phosphorus use during that period when the actual population would be smaller than the calculated population. During the sixty-three years it takes to reach a population of 12 billion, a cumulative total of 5.5 billion tons of P is consumed (always according to the 2.7 power rule). The remaining reserve of 14.5 billion tons of P (20 minus 5.5) is consumed in fifty years (14.5 billion divided by the annual use of 292 million tons). The total 20 billion supply lasts, as indicated, 113 years.

Emigh's Ore Deposit Estimates. Lines 6, 7, and 8 are based on the economic and known subeconomic deposits estimated by Emigh. For a population which stabilizes at 12 billion, the deposits of 180 billion tons of P would last on the order of 700 years, and for the 20 billion population case, they would last about 200 years. If the population simply grew at 1.9 percent per year until the entire 180 billion tons were consumed, then this amount would last about 130 years when the population would have grown to 43 billion.

Since only about 20 billion tons of Emigh's deposit total could be mined and beneficiated at current cost levels, and the remaining 160 billion tons is contained in lower-grade ore, the assumption of $50 per ton of P might be questioned. While it is certainly true that much of Emigh's estimate includes currently marginal or submarginal sources, the periods of exhaustion are long enough (100 to 700 years) that improvements in technology might compensate for these lower grades of ore. In any event, the per capita costs would still be relatively insignificant for costs double, triple, or even ten times the current cost of $50 per ton.[34]

The TIE Estimate of Ultimate Usable Deposits. Although the TIE study group might well have revised their upper limit estimate of 30 trillion tons of P contained in ores with at least 8 percent P, if they had discovered the error of a factor of 1000 in time, it may still be of some interest to determine exhaustion periods and per capita costs for various ultimate population levels. This is done on lines 9 through 12 of Table 1. Depending on the population level, exhaustion times vary between 500 and 100,000 years. Per capita costs vary between $1.22 and $45.00, based on the cost of $50 per metric ton. There is less justification for using a $50 per ton cost here, but upper limit costs are provided by the common rock estimates on lines 13 through 16, and the range between is too great to provide a meaningful estimate in the absence of data. The per ton and per capita costs for lines 9 through 12 can then be interpreted as possible lower limit costs.

Common Rock Deposits. For half the total amount of P within common rock in the top two miles (3.2 km.) of land, calculations for stable populations of 12, 20, 50, and 100 billion people are provided on lines 13 through 16. The 590 trillion tons of P does not include P in higher grades because the higher-grade deposits for which quantity estimates exist (e.g., the 180 billion tons of P identified by Emigh) are insignificant in comparison, while estimates of the quantities of P in low-grade deposits are not available. The cumulative usage of P during the period of population growth is under 0.3 percent of the total 590 trillion tons and, therefore, could have been ignored in calculating exhaustion periods for lines 13 through 16.

Run-out periods for common rock exceed six thousand years or more in all four cases. Even if environmental constraints were to limit the use of common rock to 20 percent of this total, exhaustion periods would still exceed one thousand years. Although exhaustion periods are greatly extended, per capita costs at $11,000 per ton of P are very much greater than in the lines above, especially for large world populations. But, in view of the exhaustion times involved the assumption of an $11,000 price based on current technology is probably much too high. Nevertheless, given higher income levels in the developed and underdeveloped countries over such a time span, even the extreme per capita costs tabulated might still be met.[35]

Limitations of the Calculations and Conclusions. Some additional observations should be made about Table 1. First, the results are hardly significant to the level provided. The use of the 2.7 formula would at best lead to answers with one significant digit. Additional digits have been included to provide ease of checking. The validity of the 2.7 rule is analyzed in chapters 2 and 3.

Second, even though more recent data concerning phosphorus fertilizer consumption, population size, and population growth rates are available, they were not used in order to maintain comparability with the TIE estimates. Moving from the 1968 base figures used in the TIE report to the 1971 or 1972 figures now available would not change the results very much.

Finally, for the same reason, no correction has been made for the fact that the 2.7 rule applies to crop output, not population. The 2.7 rule as related directly to population is only valid if output and population grow in proportion. If the average diet improves over time, then output will increase more than population, and the 2.7 rule based on population size alone will underestimate the projected consumption of phosphate fertilizer. The assumption in Table 1 that the average diet will not improve is adopted only to allow direct comparisons with the TIE calculations. Since it is later argued that these projections of annual P usage are much too high for populations in excess of 12 billion, little is served by increasing the estimates even further.

It is possible, of course, to make such corrections quite simply by increasing the population index by the percentage increase in per capita consumption. For example, if it is assumed that per capita agricultural consumption will increase 50 percent, then it is only necessary to increase the population 50 percent to estimate the effect. Thus, the estimated amount of P in fertilizer consumed by a population of 12 billion with a 50 percent higher per capita agricultural consumption is equivalent mathematically to that of a population of 18 billion without any increase in per capita agricultural consumption (or about 870 million tons of P per year).

The most striking thing about Table 1 is that consideration of lower-grade ores greatly extends exhaustion periods. Additional consideration such as new finds, recycling, and alternative consumption rates (yet to be discussed) will further extend these exhaustion periods. In fact, even without consideration of these factors, it is clear that the problem is not one of "running-out" or of clearly defined "exhaustion periods" but instead one of rising costs as lower and lower grades of ore are exploited.

Possible Additional Deposits and Future Costs

New Finds and Intermediate-Grade Deposits. It should be stressed again that the gap between Emigh's reserve figures of 180 billion tons of P and the ultimate, or last resort, resources of 590 trillion tons in common rock contains many thousands of millions of tons of ore in the intermediate category we have termed low-grade deposits. That is, after the 180 billion tons of phosphorus contained in higher-grade ores (8 percent P and better) are extracted, future generations will not then suddenly be forced to mine P from common rocks with an average content of 0.1 percent P.

In addition, it seems clear that Emigh's compilation of higher-grade ore deposits is quite conservative. In discussing known individual phosphate deposits he has either deliberately underestimated the reserves or left them out of the calculation because not enough was known about them.[36] Continued exploration and new finds will probably increase these totals by significant amounts. Richard Sheldon of the U.S. Geological Survey points out that:

The rapid increase in demand for phosphate has generated much exploration over the last 15 years. This exploration has been tremendously successful, with new deposits having been found in five continents—Australia, Asia, Africa, North America, and South America. In Africa, deposits have been found in Spanish Sahara, Togo, Senegal and South Africa; in Asia, Saudi Arabia, Iran, China, and the USSR; in North America, North Carolina and Mexico; and in South America, Colombia and Peru. In addition, restudy of older districts, including ones in Florida, Israel, Jordan, and Christmas Island, has greatly enlarged their reserves. . . . This exploration is still going on and more deposits, economic in today's terms, will probably be found, particularly if our exploration tools are continually sharpened by research.[37]

In a similar vein, V. E. McKelvey of the U.S. Geological Survey has commented:

Unlike many other minerals, phosphate rock has not been intensively prospected for in the past; and because it resembles limestone and other common rocks in appearance, it has not always been recognized even where it has been uncovered in the course of other work. . . . Although they are irregularly distributed, resources of phosphate rock in presently known deposits that are within reach of developed technology are probably on the order of hundreds of billions of tons.[38]

In contrast, Professor Preston Cloud of the Department of Geological Sciences at the University of California, Santa Barbara, notes that "one of the big factors leading to confidence that large *new* resources of phosphorus will be found is that we understand the geochemistry of phosphorus and have a good theory of ore-finding."[39]

In addition to the probable large additional quantities of P which are economic or near economic now but have not been discovered or adequately estimated (and, in addition, to the possibilities for recycling discussed in Chapter 4), there are even larger quantities of lower grades between the 8 percent and 0.1 percent P ores. Of course, it should not be surprising that the quantities of such reserves have not been estimated. Given commercial grade deposits of at least ninety years, with a constantly growing population, or over 1,700 years at current levels of consumption, there would not seem to be much incentive to survey or even catalog known sources that appeared to be even somewhat more expensive to mine and refine than current sources.

As Emigh points out:

There are vast areas of the continents which have not been prospected for phosphate, largely because the phosphate to be found would not be economically recoverable. It would have the required grade and mineability characteristics but could not now compete in world markets because of transportation costs. . . . There are no figures on the world's tonnage of low grade phosphatic formations. The quantities of phosphate rock that can be recovered from them will be astronomic.[40]

It would appear from this statement that not only are there large quantities of P in these low-grade deposits but the quantities may exceed those in higher-grade deposits of commercial and subeconomic ore. Phosphorus may, in fact, follow the Lasky grade-tonnage ratio rule, which states that the tonnage of the ore (but not necessarily the mineral element of interest) increases geometrically as the average grade of ore decreases arithmetically.[41] It is the total tonnage of the ore, not the contained element such as copper or phosphorus that is referred to in this Lasky ratio rule. To illustrate, assume that the cumulative tonnage of ore for some mineral at or above an ore grade of 10 percent is 40 tons, and that the cumulative amount at or above a grade level of 9 percent is 60 tons (or 1.5 times 40 tons). Then the Lasky ratio would predict that the cumulative amount of ore at or above a grade of 8 percent ore would be 90 tons (or 1.5 times 60 tons).[42]

The cumulative tonnage of metal or element contained in the ore will also increase as grade decreases but not as rapidly as the cumulative ore quantity. For example, to continue the illustration, if the mineral element contained in the 40 tons of ore with a grade of 10 percent or higher totals 6 tons, then, on the assumption the 20 tons of ore between 9 and 10 percent grade level approximately averages 9.5 percent, there are 1.95 tons of the element in this 20 tons of ore and the cumulative amount of the element contained in ores with a grade of 9 percent or better is 7.95 tons; for the 30 tons of ore lying between 8 and 9 percent grade, the amount of the mineral element contained is 2.55 tons (0.085 times 30), and the cumulative amount of the element down to the 8 percent grade level is 10.5 tons. Therefore, while the cumulative amount of ore increases by one-half for each percentage decrease in grade (from 40 to 60 to 90 tons for 10, 9, and 8 percent grades, respectively), the cumulative amount of the mineral element contained increases by less than one-half for each percentage decrease in grade (from 6 to 7.95 to 10.5 for 10, 9, and 8 percent grades, respectively).

While it might be possible to use the Lasky ratio to make estimates of the low-grade deposits of phosphorus lying above common rock but below Emigh's subeconomic deposits, the general validity of this approach has been questioned.[43] Estimates of additional quantities of P in low-grade deposits would be too speculative and would add little to our basic argument, so they have not been prepared.

Future Costs. In an analogous manner it would not be necessary to switch abruptly from phosphorus costing $50 per metric ton to P costing $11,000 per ton. Even in the absence of any technological advance, costs would simply rise slowly toward the $11,000 figure as successively lower grades (including tailings discarded from previously mined richer deposits) were used (and as recycling increased). However, improvements in technology are likely to reduce these costs significantly, including the ultimate $11,000 cost. According to McKelvey, "Advances in beneficiation and processing technology now make it possible to recover economically many lower-grade deposits that were formerly not considered mineable."[44] Sheldon argues that "large resources of marginal-grade deposits have been identified; advances in technology, if the necessary research is undertaken, will make them economic."[45]

As indicated earlier, it was on this basis that the price of the deposits totaled by Emigh was set at the current price. On the other hand, the $11,000 per ton price for P from ordinary rock is based on the existing state of the art. Since at least several centuries would pass before P would be extracted from common rocks, it is clear that this price would in all likelihood be substantially reduced by technological progress by then.

However, no reasonable way exists to project what future technology might bring. Simple, very conservative extrapolations of recent rates of change in productivity result in long-run costs that are of doubtful validity.[46] Thus, the safer course in this case is to indicate the cost based on present technology with the understanding that it is probably an upper limit.

In addition, the $11,000 per ton estimate is based on current costs of inputs as well as technology. While technology should improve, real costs of inputs (such as energy) might rise, offsetting technological improvements by some amount.

Ocean Reserves. Seawater is often suggested as a valuable source of minerals in general. However, P in its naturally occurring compounds is not very soluble in water. It is estimated that with 0.07 parts per million of P, the entire ocean contains only 99 billion metric tons.[47] An "ore" with 0.000007 percent P is not likely to be economic, even in the long run.

Most of the phosphorus in the ocean is on the sea floor rather than in the water. There are evidently vast amounts of low-grade deposits but little is known about these quantities. Most attention has been given higher-grade (about 10 percent P) phosphate "nodules." About 40 billion out of the total 160 billion tons of P included by Emigh are in the form of phosphate nodules on the sea floor of the continental shelves. This estimate reported by Emigh was made by Dr. John Mero in 1964. Emigh states Mero advised him that "phosphate nodules have since been found in many more places than were known in 1964, and the estimated reserve figure is therefore very conservative." Although there was an attempt in the early 1960s to mine some of these undersea deposits near Los Angeles, they have yet to be commercially exploited. Sheldon states:

Phosphate-rich sediments deposited in these areas [of ocean upwelling near coasts] are part of tomorrow's supply of phosphate, but the state of present technology does not favor their exploitation now, both because they are low grade and because they occur in water too deep for economic mining. Although they are not very well explored, there is no question that they constitute a very large resource.[48]

Notes

[1] The relationship between fertilizer use (Z) and crop output (W) can be stated as $W^{2.7} = k_1 Z$; the relation between crop output and population (N) is $N = k_2 W$; and the relation between fertilizer and population then becomes $N^{2.7} = k_3 Z$, or $N = (k_3 Z)^{1/2.7}$, where k_1, k_2, and k_3 are constants and $k_3 = k_1(k_2)^{2.7}$. This 2.7 rule is examined in more detail in Chapter 2 and Appendix B.

[2] As indicated in the introduction, tons refers to metric tons unless otherwise noted.

[3] The Institute of Ecology, *Man in the Living Environment*, Report of the 1971 Workshop on Global Ecological Problems (Chicago: The Institute of Ecology, 1971), p. 55. A simplified explanation of this calculation is provided in the first

section of Appendix A. This exhaustion period calculation assumes a constant annual 1.9 percent population growth rate, but in fact the rate of population growth has been very slowly increasing. According to the 1971 UN *Demographic Yearbook*, the world population is growing at 2 percent per year. Thus, a somewhat shorter exhaustion period is implied with this rate of population growth.

[4] Richard W. Lewis, "Phosphorus," in *Mineral Facts and Problems, 1970* (Washington, D.C.: Government Printing Office, 1970), p. 1143. The actual figure of 19.8 billion tons has been rounded to 20 billion tons since the estimate is not known with anything like three-significant-figure precision.

[5] The Institute of Ecology, *Man in the Living Environment*, Report of the 1971 Workshop on Global Problems, revised edition (Madison: University of Wisconsin Press, 1972), p. 55. The mechanics of this and the other calculations in this chapter are contained in Appendix A.

[6] Ibid., p. 55.

[7] This correction without reference to its source is noted in "Phosphate Reserves—Additional Information," *Phosphorus and Potassium*, No. 59 (May/June 1972), p. 8 (no author given).

[8] In some copies—but not all—of the 1972 TIE report, the three extra zeros have either been written in by hand or a correction slip has been inserted.

[9] Consumption rates for various size populations are given in the TIE report, p. 54. The exhaustion period has been simply calculated by dividing the consumption rate for a 20 billion population into the reserve of 30 trillion tons $(30 \times 10^{12}$ tons$)$.

The consumption rate for a 20 billion population can be verified by means of the 2.7 rule. For a 3.6 billion population the phosphorus use is 11.3 million tons per year, so, for a 20 billion population which is 5.556 times larger than 3.6 billion, phosphorus use must increase by $(5.556)^{2.7}$, or by a factor of about 103. Thus, a 20 billion population would use 103 times 11.3 million tons per year or about 1,160 million tons per year. The level reported in the TIE document is 1,170 million tons per year, and the discrepancy is probably due to rounding. Again, of course, none of these estimates is significant to three places but three figures are included for ease of verification.

[10] Emigh, "World Phosphate Reserves—Are There Really Enough?" *Engineering and Mining Journal* (April 1972), pp. 90–95. A similar article explicitly based in good part on Dr. Emigh's article appears in *Phosphorus and Potassium*, no. 58 (March/April 1972) entitled "Phosphate Reserves and the Ecologists: Mountain or Molehill?" (no author given), pp. 3–5, and 9.

[11] Emigh actually calculates 1.298 trillion equivalent short tons of phosphate rock containing 13.6 percent P (or 31 percent P_2O_5); 13.6 percent of 1.298 trillion short tons is about 175 billion short tons of P, or about 160 billion metric tons.

For each particular deposit Emigh converts the actual reserve quantity to the quantity of "rock" which would hold 13.6 percent P. For example, his figures indicate there are about 125 billion tons of ore with a content of 10.9 percent P (25 percent P_2O_5) in a deposit located in the country of Colombia; if this ore were beneficiated to 13.6 percent P, it would be 100 billion tons $(125 \times 10.9/13.6)$. Emigh assumes 20 percent of this would be lost in the extraction so he lists this deposit as 80 billion tons of equivalent rock containing 13.6 percent P.

It appears that well over half of the total deposits of P listed by Emigh comes from ores which contain over 8 percent P. Some of these deposits, such as those from the sea bottom or those located below ground or in distant locations, look (at this time) quite uneconomic, even though their ore grade is 8 percent P or better.

Comments on Emigh's deposit estimates by geologists and others familiar with the situation indicate that his estimates are quite conservative.

[12] TIE report, p. 53.

[13] Emigh, "World Phosphate Reserves," p. 93.

[14] Lewis, "Phosphorus," pp. 1141 and 1143.

[15] Lewis (in "Phosphorus," p. 1153) states that about 33 percent of the P is lost in these operations. In the Florida mining operations (the largest source of P in this country), the tailings contain about 5.5–7.5 percent P (ibid., p. 141) and, therefore, at some time in the future will become economic sources of phosphate. As apatite, the common phosphate mineral, is relatively insoluble in water, these tailings are evidently not dissipated away by leaching but do present (not insurmountable) environmental problems because of their form (slime) and physical land disposal requirements (ibid., p. 1149).

The phosphatic slime wastes do not naturally dry up even if left alone for several years. The present method of disposal in Florida consists of building impoundment or settling areas. About 40 thousand acres (16 thousand ha.) of settling areas exist, surrounded by about 300 miles (480 km.) of earth dams, and about 2,500 acres (1,000 ha.) of new impoundment areas are added each year. Since 1942 about twenty dam failures have occurred but improvements in design and construction are expected to reduce the rate of failure. Active research is being conducted to "dewater" the phosphatic slime wastes to reduce or avoid the need for impoundment, which still involves some risk of dam failure and which, with rising land costs and other factors, is becoming more expensive. Several methods for dewatering the slimes do exist but tend to exceed the present still very low cost of about 40 cents per ton of slime (on a dry basis, or about one or two pennies per ton on a wet basis). This information was taken from Leslie G. Bromwell, director of Florida Phosphatic Clays Research Project, "The Florida Phosphatic Clays Research Project," paper presented to The Fertilizer Industry Round Table, 23rd Annual Meeting, November 8, 1973, Washington, D.C. (mimeograph).

Since these tailings or wastes may well be utilized at a later date as a source of P, it may be legitimate to include a much higher percentage of the P in the ground as recoverable reserve; that is, to assume the amounts ultimately lost in mining and beneficiating are less than 33 percent of the in-ground phosphorus. Also, should phosphate become a much scarcer material, it can be assumed the price will go up if for no other reason than it must be extracted from lower-grade ores at a higher cost. At a higher price a higher percentage of contained P might be extracted.

[16] This concept is not new. Harrison Brown in *The Challenge of Man's Future: An Inquiry Concerning the Condition of Man During the Years That Lie Ahead* (New York: Viking Press, 1954) discusses extraction of nuclear fuels as well as minerals from common granitic rock (pp. 174–78 and 217–18).

[17] Raymond L. Parker, "Composition of the Earth's Crust," U.S. Geological Survey Professional Paper 440-D (Washington, D.C.: Government Printing Office, 1967), table 20, p. D15.

[18] A population of 50 billion would use, based on the 2.7 power rule, about 14 billion tons of P per year and would consume 5.9×10^{14} tons of P in approximately forty thousand years. A 100 billion population would use about 90 billion tons a year and would exhaust 5.9×10^{14} tons of P in about six thousand years. The fact that smaller amounts would be consumed during the earlier years when the population was still growing toward its assumed equilibrium value would have a relatively insignificant effect on extending the exhaustion period.

[19] K. B. Brown, "Recovery of Phosphate Fertilizer from Ordinary Igneous Rock," September 13, 1971, memo.

[20] H. E. Goeller, "Outline for Phosphate Resources Study" (1972), unpublished draft, p. 2. Tons refer to short tons, so the cost of P per metric ton would be about $10,000.

[21] H. E. Goeller, letter communication.

[22] Emigh comments in a letter: "Assuming a recovery of 75% of the 0.1% P content of ordinary rock into a concentrate, there would be required about 1,300 tons of rock. 1,300 tons divided into $10,000 would mean a cost of $7.50, approximately, to mine and process. This cost estimate is far too high in my opinion as it is far higher than even that which the mining industry now experiences in large-scale, open-pit mining."

[23] Robert W. Ogeton and Gertrude N. Greenspoon, "Copper," in *Mineral Facts and Problems*, p. 546.

[24] K. B. Brown points out: "No provision has been made in the costs for returning the mined rock areas to a condition that would be satisfactory. . . . Such costs are difficult to estimate, and certainly to generalize, since they depend greatly upon local circumstances."

[25] Jerome K. Delson, Richard J. Frankel, and Blair T. Bower, "Residuals Management in the Coal-Energy Industry" (draft in process, 1972), p. IV-8.

[26] E. A. Nephew, *Surface Mining and Land Reclamation in Germany*, Oak Ridge National Laboratory, ORNL-NSF-EP-16 (Oak Ridge, Tennessee; May 1972), p. 21.

[27] Delson et al., "Residuals Management," pp. IV-21 to IV-33.

[28] A population of 100 billion devouring a calculated 90,000 million tons each year would mine out the equivalent of approximately 8,000 square miles (20,000 km.²) annually. If reclamation to the German level were practiced, however, this would not necessarily be as disastrous as it might seem.

[29] Thomas S. Lovering, "Mineral Resources from the Land," in *Resources and Man*, Committee on Resources and Man of the Division of Earth Sciences, National Academy of Sciences–National Research Council (San Francisco: W. H. Freeman, 1969), p. 123.

[30] The corresponding figures for a world population of 100 billion consuming 90,000 million tons of P per year are a total cost of $990 trillion and a per capita cost of $9,900.

[31] It is difficult to imagine a world, several centuries from now, with 20 billion people most of whom having real incomes much below current U.S. levels. The cost of phosphate fertilizer would probably be an insignificant issue compared with all the other difficulties implied in that type of future.

[32] Lewis ("Phosphorus," p. 1148) estimates that the 1968 price of $45 per short ton of P might rise to $51 by the year 2000. Application of the 2.7 rule to Emigh's reserve figures on submarginal deposits would suggest very little rise in extraction costs for at least the next 200 years. All these estimates are cast in real terms; i.e., they disregard changes in the general price level. Currently (1974), of course, prices have quadrupled from this 1968 level, but this rise is probably one of the many deviations from the long-term price trend due to a short-run producing capacity shortage. If, in retrospect, $200 per ton proves to be a better estimate than $50 per ton, this would not change the main results.

[33] This figure does not include the cost of converting the phosphate into fertilizer, or delivering or applying it. Since these costs are not expected to change in real terms, they have been left out. Also, notice that the $50 price per metric ton of P does not refer to a "pure" ton of P but only a ton of P contained in enough phos-

phate rock beneficiated to a degree (on the order of 13 percent P) suitable for phosphate fertilizer manufacture. If the rock suitable for phosphate fertilizer manufacture contains an average of 13.5 percent P, then 7.4 tons of such rock costs $50 at the exit door of the beneficiation facility, which is usually near the mine.

[34] This is even more apparent if, instead of the price of beneficiated P at the mine mouth, the price of P as fertilizer delivered at the farm gate is considered. According to the 1971 edition of the FAO (Food and Agriculture Organization of the United Nations) *Production Yearbook*, vol. 25 (Rome: FAO, 1972), p. 644, the price of 100 km. of P_2O_5 in fertilizer form delivered to the U.S. farmer was $18.40 in 1970–1971. Converted to dollars per metric ton of P, this is $422 per metric ton of P (1 ton of P_2O_5 is $184, and 1 ton of P_2O_5 contains 0.4364 tons of P). The beneficiated cost of P at the mine mouth is $50 per metric ton, so processing into fertilizer and transportation adds about $372. If the cost of extracting and beneficiating P goes up from $50 to $150 per ton because of increased scarcity, this would not affect the costs of processing into fertilizer and transporting (although additional transport charges might be incurred if the eventual sources of P rock ore were located farther away from users), so the cost of P to the farmer would be increased from $422 to $522 per ton. Thus, a tripling of the beneficiated mine mouth cost of P (from $50 to $150) increases the farmer's cost by only 24 percent.

[35] A contrasting view is expressed by Lovering ("Mineral Resources From the Land," p. 130): "When the time comes for living in a society dependent on scrap for high grade metal and on common rocks for commercial ore, the affluent society will be much overworked to maintain a standard of living equal to *that of a century ago*." (Italics supplied.) Brown (*The Challenge of Man's Future*) disagrees and cites estimated costs for extracting uranium and thorium from granite (pp. 174–78), and argues as well that metallic minerals might also be extracted at the same time (pp. 217–18).

[36] V. E. McKelvey, director of the U.S. Geological Survey, notes in a letter that "Emigh's report does not mention all of the promising known deposits—Angola, for example—and his list of areas that 'contain known reserves which cannot be quantified now' include several with high-grade deposits that are being mined now. His report is indeed a conservative one. . . ."

[37] Richard P. Sheldon, "World Phosphate Resources," *Mining Congress Journal*, vol. 55, no. 2 (February 1969), pp. 115–118.

[38] V. E. McKelvey, "Phosphate Deposits," U.S. Geological Survey Bulletin 1252-D (Washington, D.C.: Government Printing Office, 1967).

[39] P. E. Cloud, letter communication. He notes parenthetically that his statement holds for phosphorus and a few other elements only.

[40] Emigh, "World Phosphate Reserves," pp. 92 and 95.

[41] S. G. Lasky, "How Tonnage and Grade Relationships Help Predict Ore Reserves," *Engineering and Mining Journal*, vol. 151 (1950), pp. 81–85.

[42] In mathematical terms, $K = a/r^G$; where K is the cumulative amount of ore at or above ore grade level of G; r is the geometric factor; and a is a constant. For our example above, r is 1.5 and a is $40 \cdot (1.5)^{10}$.

[43] For somewhat contrasting views see David B. Brooks, "The Lead-Zinc Anomaly," *SME Transactions*, Society of Mining Engineers, vol. 238 (June 1967), pp. 129–136 and Lovering, "Mineral Resources from the Land," pp. 112–117. Brooks argues against discontinuities in aggregate grade-tonnage relationships, but Lovering warns that "the A/G [Lasky] ratio applies only to certain individual deposits and not to ore deposits in general, . . . [and] it should not be used in estimating the unfound reserves of a region or a nation."

[44] McKelvey, as cited by Emigh, "World Phosphate Reserves," p. 92.

[45] Sheldon, "World Phosphate Resources," p. 117.

[46] The answers may also appear unbelievable. If productivity increases fast enough to reduce the real cost 1 percent per year (a very conservative rate by comparison with twentieth-century experience), then in a thousand years the cost would only be about 50 cents per ton. While it would be presumptuous to claim this could not happen over such a time span (by that time highly sophisticated machines could be doing most of the work), it is not a figure that is easy to defend.

[47] *Marine Resources and Legal-Political Arrangements for Their Development*, Panel Reports of the Commission on Marine Science, Engineering and Resources, vol. 3 (Washington, D.C.: Government Printing Office, 1969), p. VII-102.

[48] Sheldon, "World Phosphate Resources," p. 117.

2

Projection Formulas
for Fertilizer Consumption

The 2.7 Power Rule

Since the 2.7 exponential rule is basic to the estimate of future consumption, and since such exponential projections are commonly used in analyzing the adequacy of various sorts of resources, an examination of its background and validity in this case is summarized here (and discussed in more detail in Appendix B).

The 2.7 rule is introduced in the TIE report as follows:

An empirical study of the relation between fertilizer input and agricultural yield shows that fertilizer use must increase 2.7 times more rapidly than the increase in yield. Assuming that the present level of food per person is a minimal goal for the future, we can conclude from this that the use of fertilizers must increase at least 2.7 times faster than the population.[1]

Figure 1 illustrates this relationship. (The curve entitled "Modified FAO Equation" will be discussed later in this chapter; both curves are based on the entries in Table 3 at the end of the chapter.) The 2.7 rule curve shows that to double the population (say, from 50 to 100 billion) requires much more than a doubling of phosphorus fertilizer (and other inputs) to maintain diets at their present (inadequate) levels, so the relationship is referred to as a diminishing marginal yield relationship.

The TIE report finds that recent statistics on the growth of population and the use of phosphate fertilizer conform to this 2.7 rule; i.e.,

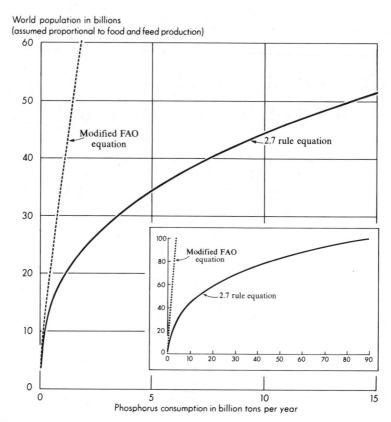

World population in billions
(assumed proportional to food and feed production)

Phosphorus consumption in billion tons per year

FIGURE 1.   Projections of Phosphorus Consumption as a Function of Population and Food Production

recent annual world population growth has been about 1.9 percent and phosphate fertilizer consumption growth about 5.25 percent, or a 2.76 percent increase in phosphate fertilizer consumption per 1 percent increase in population size.[2]

However, the origin of the rule is somewhat casual. It is based on a regression analysis of only nine data points—all fertilizer usage per hectare versus crop yields per hectare for three countries at three times.[3] The regression also implies that fertilizer alone is responsible for crop output, and other inputs such as irrigation, weeding, climate, soil, and pesticides do not matter. Although there is close correlation among some of the inputs—increased use of fertilizer is usually accompanied by increased use of pesticide, for example—this does not change the fundamental problem of determining how output per hectare increases as fertilizer is increased or even what the optimal set of inputs might be under certain price conditions (e.g., high phosphorus prices). Furthermore, the countrywide averages used may disguise important details.

Finally, the regression is based on annual yields up to 5,000 kg. per hectare (in Japan). Assuming that 20 percent of the yields are lost in processing and that each kilogram of processed crop grain contains about 3,000 calories, the net annual processed production per hectare of 4,000 kg. yields 12 million calories. Assuming that 1.5 million calories per year (4,110 calories per day) are needed for each person for all crops—agricultural and industrial crops as well as feed crops used for animal production—then about eight persons per arable hectare could be supported with an annual output of 5,000 kg. of grain per hectare. If all 1,424 million currently arable hectares[4] were to yield this level of output, they could support about 11 billion people. Thus, extrapolating the 2.7 rule to a population of 20 billion, as the TIE study does, may be invalid. It is even more doubtful that the 2.7 rule calculation has any validity in projecting phosphorus usage for the larger populations of 50 and 100 billion as we have done in Table 1 in Chapter 1.

The Modified FAO Fertilizer Prediction Formula

The same study from which the 2.7 rule was taken contains a more extensive analysis of yields versus fertilizer consumption per hectare.[5] Although it suffers many of the drawbacks of the 2.7 rule, many more data points were used. This fertilizer study is actually a revision of a 1962 FAO analysis by Williams and Couston for predicting fertilizer needs in less-developed nations.[6]

Williams and Couston plotted the average "yield-value index" of crop production per arable hectare against average inorganic fertilizer use in kilograms per arable hectare for forty-one countries in the 1956–58 period. The yield-value index is a value measure of agricultural output for food and nonfood crops. Fertilizer is defined, as is standard, in terms of the weight of nitrogen (N), phosphate (P_2O_5) and potash (K_2O). Williams and Couston fitted to these data the function $V = 77.62 + 0.1553F + 14.30F^{\frac{1}{2}}$, where V is the annual yield-value index per hectare and F is the annual fertilizer use in kilograms per hectare. The coefficient of determination (R^2) for this equation is 0.83, which is quite impressive considering that no other explanatory variables are included in the equation and that the climate and soil conditions among countries vary considerably. They point out, of course, that increased fertilizer use is usually accompanied by increases in other inputs, as well as by modern methods, so that, as in the 2.7 power rule case, attribution of increased yields to increased fertilizer usage alone would be incorrect.

The PSAC Adaption of the FAO Equation.   Nelson and Ewell, who conducted the fertilizer study for the PSAC report, adapted the FAO formula for estimating additional fertilizer consumption as food production increased in the less-developed regions by certain levels. The regression equation, for reasons that are not explained, is changed to $V = 85.04 + 0.2496F + 12.51\,F^{\frac{1}{2}}$ in their analysis. The average yield-value index per hectare of arable land (V) and the average fertilizer use per hectare of arable land (F) are determined individually for each country for the 1961–63 period, so they may have simply reestimated the curve with these more recent data.

To project the fertilizer consumption for any given country, if food output were to increase by, say, 50 percent, the yield-value index was increased by 50 percent, and the average fertilizer usage rate was determined from the equation given above. The total estimated fertilizer consumption was then calculated by multiplying the usage per arable hectare rate by the total existing number of arable hectares. Increases of 10, 25, 50, and 100 percent were calculated for twenty less-developed nations and three other less-developed regions. Totals were cumulated for each level of increase; thus, a total 25 percent increase in the food supply of the less-developed countries was assumed to consist of a 25 percent increase in each country included. A final minor adjustment shifted the base period from 1961–63 to 1966.

Application to Aggregate Data. In order to contrast the 2.7 rule with the Nelson and Ewell modified form of the FAO equation, it is first necessary to determine whether the modified FAO equation could be applied to the aggregate data rather than to each country alone as done in the PSAC study. For this purpose, I used the data from the PSAC study.

The total fertilizer usage for the less-developed countries and regions was divided by the total arable land involved to derive an average annual fertilizer usage rate of 4.8 kg. per arable hectare (3.315 million metric tons per year divided by 689 million ha.). This value of F was substituted into the modified FAO formula to determine the average yield-value index of 113.7. To calculate the amount of fertilizer associated with a 100 percent increase in the yield-value index, the latter was doubled to a value of 227.4, and from this the corresponding F (about 91 kg. of fertilizer per hectare) was determined.[7]

At an average annual rate of fertilizer consumption of 91 kg. of fertilizer per arable hectare, total annual consumption for the area involved (689 million arable ha.) would be 63 million tons of fertilizer. In contrast, the annual amount of fertilizer estimated by Nelson and Ewell for a country-by-country doubling of the yield-value index is 57 million tons. The estimate, using the data in an aggregate form, yields a fertilizer consumption rate 10 percent higher, a difference which would seem to be acceptable, especially for our purposes, since the aggregate approach provides a higher rather than lower value.

This test was also applied to the PSAC data with a 1966 base. In this instance Nelson and Ewell calculate that the annual fertilizer consumption must increase from 6.15 million tons to 67 million tons per year for a 100 percent increase in the yield-value index for each country and area included. The aggregated data approach indicates that a doubling of the yield-value index is associated with an annual fertilizer consumption of 80 million tons instead of 67 million tons. The difference in this case is 20 percent, but, again, this is acceptable since the aggregate approach indicates larger quantities of fertilizer consumption.

Revised FAO Formula Fertilizer Predictions

The results of applying the modified FAO formula to aggregate data are summarized in Table 2, which follows the same format as Table 1.[8] As in all lines of Table 1, except the first two, an initial world population of 3.6 billion, a population growth rate of 1.9 percent per year, and an initial world consumption level of 11.3 million metric tons of phosphorus are used.

As the FAO formula relates to total processed fertilizer use in terms of metric tons of nitrogen (N), phosphorus pentoxide (P_2O_5), and potash (K_2O), it was necessary to determine what fraction of this would be phosphorus. The simple assumption was made that the 1968–69 ratio would hold; in fact, the ratio of phosphate fertilizer to total fertilizer use has been declining slowly but steadily since the mid-1950s, mainly because of increased use of nitrogen fertilizer. In the fiscal year 1954–55, P_2O_5 was 40 percent of all fertilizer consumed as measured by the combined weight of P_2O_5, N, and K_2O; in 1961–62 this ratio declined to 36 percent; and in 1969–70 reached 32 percent.[9] During the fiscal 1968–69 period, the ratio of processed phosphorus fertilizer (including ground rock and phosphorus fertilizer used in Mainland China, North Vietnam, and North Korea) to the corresponding total of N, P_2O_5, and K_2O was 0.138.[10] This figure was used to estimate the amounts of P consumed annually per hectare in the modified FAO formula.

This annual quantity of P per hectare was then multiplied by 1.424 billion ha.[11] to obtain the estimated total annual amount of inorganic P fertilizer used.

Since this quantity of P represents P used in fertilizer production while the figures used in the revised TIE report are mining production data, the annual amount of inorganic P fertilizer applied was increased by about 28 percent to be representative of production figures. The details of this adjustment are contained in Appendix A.

For an annual average worldwide use of about 45 kg. of fertilizer (in terms of N, P_2O_5, and K_2O) per arable hectare,[12] the corresponding yield-value index is 180.2. It was assumed that the yield-value index, V, moved in proportion to population. If the population increased from 3.6 billion to, for example, 7.2 billion, it was correspondingly assumed that V also would double to a value of 360.4. With a yield-value index of 360.4, about 274 kg. of fertilizer per arable hectare per year would be used, according to the revised FAO formula.[13]

As indicated in Appendix B, the assumption that agricultural output per capita remains constant has not held true in the past and may not hold true in the future, especially since most people have inadequate diets. For the world as a whole, much less increase in per capita output will probably take place once the less-developed countries catch up. Although correction for this factor could easily be incorporated into the analysis,[14] it has not been done in order to maintain comparability with the TIE estimates in Table 1. Instead, it has been assumed that any given percentage increase must only be matched by the same percentage increase in the yield-value index.

By comparison with Table 1 it can be seen in Table 2 that "exhaustion" periods are approximately the same for small reserves and small populations but are substantially lengthened for larger reserve figures. For these latter cases, annual consumption rates and costs are also decreased by a large amount. For ease of comparison, annual total and per capita production rates for various world population sizes are shown in Table 3 and Figure 1 (annual totals only in Figure 1). Since the values in Table 2 are based on a formula derived from a much more extensive data analysis than those in Table 1 (although both projection equations were derived for estimating fertilizer needs in less-developed countries rather than for extrapolating fertilizer consumption for much larger world population levels), there at least exist some grounds for giving greater credence to the results of Table 2.[15]

Even though the figures derived from the FAO formula deserve greater credibility, there still remain serious questions about projections beyond certain population levels. The FAO curve was plotted from data extending to yield-value indices of about 500. Therefore, fertilizer calculations from a doubling or tripling of the existing average yield-value index of 180 might be acceptable but results for extrapolations above this level are clearly suspect. This means that the fer-

TABLE 2. Exhaustion Periods and Per Capita Costs for Phosphorus Derived from the Modified FAO Formula

Source of deposit estimate and case number	Average grade of ore (% P) (1)	Recoverable amounts of P (billion tons) (2)	Ultimate population (billions) (3)	Annual use of P at ultimate population level (million tons) (4)	Total years to exhaustion (5)	At ultimate population level (Col. 3)		
						Annual consumption of P per person (kg.) (Col. 4 ÷ Col. 3) (6)	Price ($/ton) (7)	Annual per capita cost ($/person) (Col. 6 × Col. 7 ÷ 1,000) (8)
Current and subeconomic deposits								
TIE revised								
1	12	20	3.6[a]	11.3	1,750	3.1	50	0.16
2	12	20	26.8	634.0	106	23.6	50	1.18
3	12	20	12	181.0	150	15.1	50	0.75
4	12	20	20	412.0	110	20.6	50	1.03
Emigh								
5	8	180	12	181.0	1,040	15.1	(50)[b]	(0.75)[b]
6	8	180	20	412.0	498	20.6	(50)	(1.03)
7	8	180	50	1,470.0	225	29.4	(50)	(1.47)
8	8	180	100	3,470.0	187	34.7	(50)	(1.74)
Long-run and common rock deposits								
TIE revised								
9	8	30,000	12	181.0	166,000	15.1	(50)	(0.75)
10	8	30,000	20	412.0	72,900	20.6	(50)	(1.03)
11	8	30,000	50	1,470.0	20,500	29.4	(50)	(1.47)
12	8	30,000	100	3,470.0	8,780	34.7	(50)	(1.74)
Common rock								
13	0.1	590,000	12	181.0	3,260,000	15.1	11,000	166.00
14	0.1	590,000	20	412.0	1,430,000	20.6	11,000	226.00
15	0.1	590,000	50	1,470.0	402,000	29.4	11,000	323.00
16	0.1	590,000	100	3,470.0	170,000	34.7	11,000	382.00

[a] Based on 1968 world population.
[b] The price and cost figures in parentheses are to be interpreted as lower bound estimates.

TABLE 3. Comparisons of the Annual Phosphorus Production Rates Predicted by the 2.7 Rule and the Modified FAO Formula

World population (billions)	Annual production of P (million tons)		Annual per capita production of P (kg.)	
	2.7 rule	FAO formula	2.7 rule	FAO formula
3.6[a]	11.3[a]	11.3[a]	3.1	3.1
12.0	292.0	181.0	24.3	15.1
20.0	1,160.0	412.0	57.9	20.6
50.0	13,750.0	1,470.0	275.0	29.4
100.0	89,300.0	3,470.0	893.0	34.7

[a] Current (1968) population and usage (production) of P.

tilizer consumption rates calculated for populations in excess of 12 billion are probably inaccurate even for the FAO equation.[16]

Notes

[1] The Institute of Ecology, *Man in the Living Environment*, Report of the 1971 Workshop on Global Problems, revised edition (Madison: University of Wisconsin Press, 1972), p. 55.

[2] Ibid.

[3] As outlined in Appendix B, this 2.7 rule was developed by a group primarily concerned with projecting pesticide needs in less-developed countries: see W. B. Ennis et al., "Inputs for Pesticides" in the President's Science Advisory Committee (PSAC), Panel on the World Food Supply, *The World Food Problem* (Washington: Government Printing Office, 1967), vol. III, pp. 139–145. The description of this projection formula is taken from the PSAC study.

[4] Food and Agriculture Organization (FAO), *Production Yearbook: 1970*, vol. 24 (Rome: FAO, 1971), table 1. This is the reported arable land including land under permanent crops.

[5] Lewis B. Nelson and Raymond H. Ewell, "Fertilizer Requirements for Increased Food Needs," *The World Food Problem*, (PSAC) vol. III, pp. 95–103. This analysis by Nelson and Ewell, even though contained in the same PSAC volume in which the 2.7 rule is derived, was done independently. The two methods are not compared in the PSAC study, particularly since the 2.7 formula is really derived as a minor by-product in attempting to project pesticide usage. (Ennis et al. merely wished to point out that agricultural output, fertilizer usage and pesticide usage were all correlated so that, for example, pesticide usage and output might be predicted from fertilizer data alone.)

According to a letter from Frederick E. Smith of Harvard University, who was involved in preparing the TIE report, the TIE panel did compare the two approaches and "found the [2.7] power function easier to use, noted that they were very similar but did not examine their discrepancy when greatly extrapolated" [evidently beyond a world population of 12 billion]. A plot of the relationship between fertilizer usage and agricultural output derived by Nelson and Ewell is reproduced on p. 16 of the TIE report.

[6] Moyle S. Williams and John W. Couston, *Crop Production Levels and Fertilizer Use* (Rome: FAO, 1962). Also see Frank W. Parker, "Fertilizer and Economic Development," in Malcolm H. McVickar, G. L. Bridger, and Lewis B. Nelson, eds., *Fertilizer Technology and Usage* (Madison, Wisconsin: Soil Science Society of America, 1963), pp. 1–22.

[7] Given $V = 85.04 + 0.2496F + 12.51F^{\frac{1}{2}}$, if F equals 4.811, then V equals 113.68. If V equals 227.36 then F equals approximately 91.3.

[8] Calculation equations are explained in Appendix A.

[9] Data from various annual editions of FAO, *Fertilizers: An Annual Review of World Production, Consumption and Trade* (Rome). The 1970 edition of this annual was renamed *Annual Fertilizer Review: 1970*. Totals for P_2O_5 and total P_2O_5, N, and K_2O include the minor amounts of ground rock phosphate applied directly without processing in a fertilizer plant but exclude the (also minor) amounts used in Mainland China, North Vietnam, and North Korea because data for these countries extend back only a few years.

[10] FAO, *Annual Fertilizer Review: 1970*, pp. 29, 33, and 37. The total amount of processed fertilizer consumed in terms of N, P_2O_5 and K_2O during 1968–69 was reported as 60.659 million metric tons, including 1.22 million tons of ground phosphate rock used directly without further processing and 3.079 million tons of fertilizer used in Mainland China, North Vietnam, and North Korea. The total amount of P_2O_5 fertilizer for this period is reported as 19.117 million metric tons including the 1.22 million tons of P_2O_5 in phosphate rock used directly and 0.497 million tons of P_2O_5 used in China, etc. This 19.117 million tons of P_2O_5 contains 8.343 million tons of P, and the ratio of 8.343 to 60.659 is 0.138.

[11] FAO, *Production Yearbook: 1970*, vol. 24 (Rome: FAO, 1971), table 1. This is the reported amount of arable land in the world including land under permanent crops for 1969. The 1969 land figures are probably a more accurate estimate than the 1968 figures because in many countries the data reported on land use lag behind actual use patterns (ibid., p. 700).

[12] FAO, *Annual Fertilizer Review: 1970*, table 12. China, North Vietnam and North Korea, plus all phosphate rock used directly as fertilizer, were excluded from this calculation. After allowing for these, the average drops to 44.8 kg. per hectare. No correction for this difference was made since it is small and the data unreliable in any event.

[13] In the actual calculations the value of F of 45 kg. per hectare was directly associated with a world production value of P of 11.3 million tons per year. When V was increased, F was determined, and it was simply assumed that the world production of P increased in proportion to F.

[14] The yield-value index would merely be increased by the percentage increase in the agricultural output per capita. Based on existing data, the necessary increase to bring the world calorie intake from the 1964–66 level of about 2,400 calories per capita a day to (the perhaps excessive) U.S. levels of about 3,200 calories per capita per day, would be about 33 percent. Data taken from FAO, *The State of Food and Agriculture: 1972* (Rome: FAO, 1972), p. 24; and FAO, *Production Yearbook: 1971*, p. 443.

[15] As indicated in footnote 5, the TIE panel merely used the 2.7 rule as an approximation to the more mathematically complex FAO formula.

[16] The very large increases above current levels in the annual consumption of phosphorus fertilizer for the larger populations, even as predicted by the FAO

formula (Table 3) bring into question whether the environmental strains of such levels of usage could be tolerated. Since the amounts of nitrogen and potassium fertilizer would also be increased, these environmental problems would be further multiplied. While these pollution problems (as well as others) might very well limit the ultimate population level, we merely cite the possibility at this point. However, recycling and erosion control are relevant to the environmental damages from phosphorus consumption, and these are briefly touched upon (primarily from the point of view of conserving P) in chapters 3 and 4.

3

A Fertilizer
Usage Function Based
On Physical Considerations

It is helpful to contrast the actual phosphorus fertilizer usage of certain fairly densely populated (in terms of arable land) nations, such as Japan and the Netherlands, against the amounts predicted by the 2.7 and FAO rules. A detailed analysis of P usage in such countries, provided in Appendix C, indicates that the two rules evidently overpredict the amount of P fertilizer applied each year. The formulas may be quite acceptable for predictive purposes in lower-density countries, but this is of little concern here because, as world population increases, population densities will be higher, and if the world population does not become as large as the numbers used in Tables 1 and 2, then the calculated exhaustion periods are even greater than indicated.

Multiple-Crop Experiments

The discrepancy between the formula predictions of fertilizer usage and the actual rate in Taiwan is particularly large (see Table C-1 in Appendix C), and this is probably due to double and triple cropping practiced there. Few of the other countries examined in Appendix C begin to approach the level of multicropping used in Taiwan. Allocating 20 kg. of P over two or three crops in a single hectare per year is likely to bring about much more output than allocating the 20 kg.

36

to a single crop because of the diminishing returns from fertilizer applications.

Such multicropping practices are probably going to play an increasingly important role in supporting higher population densities.[1] In looking ahead 100 or more years (as in Tables 1 and 2) it would seem reasonable to assume that currently advanced crop production techniques will become standard practice by then. For this reason it is pertinent to consider experimental field trials of multiple cropping.

The most significant drawback of using such experiments as examples is that the results may be too highly localized. That is, the use of whole countries tends to bring about more averaging of weather and soil conditions, while utilization of results from a few hectares of land in a particular location may be open to the criticism that the local soil and weather conditions are not very typical of large areas. Nevertheless, these results are probably indicative of what may be accomplished eventually. In addition, the striking and counterintuitive results found by Williams and Couston, originators of the FAO formula, that differences in weather and soils among countries did not seem to play an important part in explaining crop yield differences, are worth mentioning as a factor in giving credence to field trials.[2] In the long run, poor soils and poor climates may be overcome without extensive additions to fertilizer usage or without significant declines in yields.[3]

Bradfield's Experiments. In a multiple-crop experiment conducted by Richard Bradfield at the International Rice Research Institute in the Philippines, 22.5 metric tons of grain per hectare were produced in one year.[4] This consisted of 5 tons of rice and 17.6 tons of sorghum (three crops of sorghum). After allowances for processing and waste, this is equivalent to about 60 million calories per hectare per year.[5] Average yields may have been somewhat below this level, and inclusion of soybeans and other vegetables in the crop rotation would also have reduced this calorie production rate, but these factors are probably not enough to reduce the average annual production rate below 50 million calories per hectare. At a per capita calorie consumption rate of 1.5 million calories per year (4,100 calories per day), thirty or forty people could be supported by each arable hectare, or a total of about 50 billion people on the assumption that crops can be grown year-round on all existing arable land of 1,400 million ha.[6]

The per capita consumption of 1.5 million calories per year includes some animal feed and industrial crops (e.g., cotton) as well as directly consumed foods. Although 1.5 million calories per year is probably well above the existing world average, and may be quite adequate, it is far short of the existing U.S. level of about 3 million calories per year, most of which is used to feed animals to provide meat and animal products (milk and eggs).[7] While the heavy concentration of meat and animal products in the U.S. diet may not even be healthful for us, the number of persons who could be supported at this level from a single hectare supplying 50 million calories per year is fifteen or twenty.

According to Bradfield, between 50 and 100 kg. of P_2O_5 (22 to 44 kg. of P) were applied per hectare for each crop.[8] For four crops per year, this is 176 kg. of P per hectare (4 $\times$ 44) to produce 50 million calories. If this supports thirty people per hectare, the per capita usage would be 6 kg. of P per year—well below the levels predicted by either projection method in Table 3. For a U.S. standard, with only fifteen people supported by each hectare, the annual per capita usage of 12 kg. of P is still below those predicted levels.

De Wit's Theoretical Agricultural Output Limits

C. T. De Wit, a professor of theoretical crop husbandry at the Agricultural University at Wageningen in the Netherlands, examined the demands for fertilizer in considering the ultimate "carrying" capacity of the earth.[9] He points out that, without fertilizers and other industrialized inputs, annual agricultural production could be (and, before their introduction in the nineteenth century, was, in the more advanced nations) about 2,000 kg. (2 tons) of grain per hectare. At a rate of 3 calories per gram of grain at the consumption point, this is equivalent to 6 million calories, enough to support four people per year at the level of 1.5 million calories per person. With 1,400 million arable ha., the total population could be about 8 billion people, which is to be contrasted with the TIE estimate of 1 to 2 billion. Even at an annual 3 million calories per person (the U.S. level), two people per hectare, or 3 billion people, could be supported with no increase in the amount of arable land.[10]

Maximum Food Production.   More relevant are De Wit's calculations on the upper limits of global food production and population levels. Based on maximum photosynthesis rates, and actual average light intensities in the Netherlands, he calculates that, after allowance for nonedible portions, the maximum production from a single crop of cereal grain is about 10 tons per hectare, and 100 tons per hectare from potatoes. To support these estimates, he notes that, for cereal grains, the average production in the Netherlands is 5 tons per hectare, but good and lucky farmers may reach up to 8 tons and, on experimental fields, yields of over 9 tons per hectare have been obtained. For potatoes, the comparable figures are an average of close to 40 tons; on good farms 60–70 tons; and, experimentally, a yield of 100 tons per hectare (near the theoretical limit) has been obtained.[11]

Beyond this, De Wit believes that for the Netherlands "it is not unreasonable to suppose that with our present knowledge and our present crops it is possible to obtain [evidently through multiple cropping] . . . 12,500 kg. [12.5 tons] organic material per hectare per year in a form suitable for human consumption, . . . [or] a quantity of energy of 50 million kilocalories per hectare per year. . . ."[12] He estimates that for the tropics, where the sunlight received is greater and the growing season longer, about 30 tons of edible organic matter or 120 million calories could be grown each year on each arable hectare.[13]

To make a complete calculation of potential world food production, he estimates the potential production for each 10-degree band of land by latitude ranging from 70 degrees North to 50 degrees South, a total of thirteen bands. Assuming that each person lives on a vegetable diet of 1 million calories per year, or 2,740 calories per day, and that *all* land between latitude 70 North and 50 South (13,100 million hectares) is cultivated, De Wit calculates that about one trillion (10^{12}) people could be supported.

While it is possible to argue over the first assumption, it is the second which would seem to conflict most with the observable facts, since only about 10 percent of the land surface of the world is now cultivated. However, the amount of arable land is probably more a function of cost than technological constraints. At higher costs many lands such as deserts and tundra might be made to grow crops.[14]

In any event, the validity of this assumption is not critical since De Wit points out factors which would tend to constrain world population size. He calculates that to have a better diet with meat included, 2 million calories per year and, therefore, twice as much land per person would be needed, so the potential population would be reduced to 500 billion people. Considerations of desirable levels of living space lead him to conclude that world populations of 75 to 130 billion people would, or at least should be, the upper limit levels.[15]

Fertilizer Inputs for High-Level Agriculture. Although De Wit's observations on population size limits are relevant to our assumptions about population sizes, the more significant aspects of De Wit's analysis are those concerning fertilizer and other inputs for high-yield agriculture:

Phosphate is indispensable for a high yield level. It appears in the many potential yield experiments that have been done during the last ten years that the present phosphate level and phosphate fertilization rates are more than sufficient to achieve the highest possible yields. Obviously an increase in yield per unit area does not necessarily lead to an increase in the use of phosphate. . . . High yields also lead to the use of less nitrogen fertilizer per unit product. The yield per unit of water is also the highest in high yielding situations. . . . The amount of biocides used per unit of product also decreases in proportion to the increase in yields.

The situation may be summarized as follows. With moderate yield levels large amounts of agricultural land are needed to feed the millions and this leads to the use of considerable quantities of fertilizer, biocides and water per unit product, to the establishment of a huge industry for manufacturing, collecting and processing all these materials and to the practical impossibility of controlling their diffusion throughout the remnants of a more or less natural vegetation. On the other hand, with a high yield level far less agricultural land is needed and far less fertilizer, biocides and water are necessary per unit of product, a smaller industry suffices to cover these needs and it is at least less difficult to control the diffusion of contaminants throughout the much larger areas that are still covered with more or less natural vegetation.[16]

Based on this interpretation, the very large per capita quantities of P per year, projected in tables 1 and 2 by the use of the two formulas, are not likely to be necessary in the long run. The corresponding exhaustion times would, therefore, be greatly extended and the per capita costs greatly reduced.

Ultimate Lower Limits of Per Capita Phosphorus Consumption

The dry organic matter of plants contains by weight an average of about 0.5 percent phosphorus, with an approximate range from 0.1 to 1 percent.[17] Since this represents the amount of P removed from the soil and incorporated into the plant, it is the amount (aside from other losses from the soil) that commercial fertilizer is intended to replace. For a direct and indirect consumption of 1.5 million calories per year (4,100 calories per day) per person, about 500 kg. of edible crops would be needed (3,000 calories per kg. after processing), or 1,000 kg. of total crops per year since only half of cereal crops are edible. Assuming a high level of P content of 1 percent, this 1,000 kg. of crops would require 10 kg. of P. With 3 million calories per year per person (the U.S. figure), 2,000 kg. of total crops, or 20 kg. of P, per person would be used annually.

Not all this need be in inorganic processed fertilizer form. Part could be supplied from animal manure and wastes, and from composts. Part of the nonedible crops could be left on the soil to supply nutrients also, and some could be fed to animals so that less than 1 or 2 tons of crops per person per year would be consumed. The estimate is also high because the 1 percent P content of dry plant matter is generally an upper limit rather than an average.

On the other hand, this 10 to 20 kg. estimate includes no provision for losses of P from soil runoff, erosion, and leaching. One of the assumptions underlying this estimate is that most such losses would have to be prevented. (A brief discussion of the factors involved and a cost estimate concerning soil erosion losses is contained in Appendix D.) For one fairly favorable case study, the cost per ton of P saved from erosion is very crudely estimated to be on the order of $500. Under less favorable conditions or different assumptions, costs might be several times this. When considered against the cost of P from common rock (as high as $11,000 per ton) a high level of erosion control may be preferable, especially when the usual benefits of erosion control—maintaining a good agricultural top soil and preventing runoff pollution—are also included.

Another important assumption, discussed briefly in Appendix D, is that most of the phosphate fertilizer applied to the soil becomes chemically "fixed" and then slowly (in some cases over a period of twenty years or more) becomes available to the plants growing there. However, since very long periods of hundreds or thousands of years are being considered here, the fact that it might even take as long as 100 years for plants to utilize a major fraction of any given dosage of phosphorous fertilizer would not seem to invalidate the analysis.

When all of these various factors are considered together, 10 to 20 kg. of P per capita per year still might be a rather conservative lower limit; even lower limits might be achieved. The data on annual usage of commercial P fertilizer per capita in Japan and the Netherlands, reported in Appendix C, indicate that the 10 to 20 kg. estimate may be somewhat high, even with conventional levels of soil erosion control and existing farming practices. Annual per capita doses of about 7 kg. of P seem adequate in these well-fed, but rather densely populated countries.[18] In comparison, the revised FAO formula does seem to yield predictions not too much higher; i.e., 20 or 30 kg. of P per capita per year for large populations (Table 3).

An Alternative Interpretation of the Lower Limit Estimate.   It is possible to look at the per capita estimate of 10 to 20 kg. of P a year as a limiting value under somewhat different assumptions. If a more realistic average P content of plants of 0.5 percent were used, then only 5 or 10 kg. per year would be needed. This could be further lowered if the nonedible plant portions were returned to the soil directly, or indirectly through manure. It could also be lowered if crops with greater edible portions were substituted. Assuming 5 or 10 kg. of P is removed by crops, then additional losses of P from soil erosion, fixation, and other sources can be as large as 5 or 10 kg. and still the annual per capita requirement would not exceed 10 to 20 kg.[19]

Thus, given the nature of the derivation, an annual per capita usage of 10 or 20 kg. of P would seem to be a reasonable estimate if the price of phosphate begins to rise significantly. Since a growing scarcity of phosphorus implies such a price rise, actual use would begin to approach such a limit if scarcity did threaten. Although this level does exceed actual rates in advanced but densely populated countries, at significantly higher population levels more intensive farming might require higher levels of per capita fertilizer use.

Nevertheless, the substitution for the 2.7 rule estimates of an upper limit of 10 to 20 kg. of P per year would substantially lengthen the exhaustion periods for the larger populations indicated in Table 1. The 2.7 rule would seem to be completely invalid in the long run for populations in excess of 10 billion, if the above reasoning is correct. A 20 kg. "rule" would yield results quite similar to those in Table 2, which are based on the FAO formula.

Notes

[1] In the short run, this will mainly be restricted to tropical and subtropical countries with favorable climates. In the very long run, use of waste heat, etc., could also allow more multiple cropping in countries with less favorable climates.

[2] Moyle S. Williams and John W. Couston, *Crop Production Levels and Fertilizer Use* (Rome: FAO, 1962), pp. 3–9.

[3] This must be so since at the extreme it is possible to grow crops without any soil and in practically any weather at all—as in soilless horticulture, hydroponics, within heated greenhouses.

[4] Richard Bradfield, "Training Agronomists for Increasing Food Production in the Humid Tropics," in J. Ritchie Cowan and L. S. Robertson, eds., *International Agronomy: Training and Education*, ASA Special Publication Number 15 (Madison, Wisconsin: American Society of Agronomy, Inc., 1969), p. 60.

[5] The 5 tons of rough rice are assumed to be converted to 3.25 tons (3,250 kg.) of milled rice (5.0 × 0.65). Each kilogram of milled rice is assumed to contain 3,600 calories for a total of 11.7 million calories. The sorghum was reduced by 20 percent to allow for processing. With 3,430 calories per kilogram, the 17.6 tons of sorghum

convert to 48.3 million calories (17.6 × 0.80 × 3,430 × 10³). The conversion ratios and calorie contents were taken from Charlotte Chatfield, *Food Composition Tables for International Use* (Washington: FAO, October 1949), pp. 9–10. Conversion to edible products is necessary to derive estimates of supportable populations.

[6] As discussed in Chapter 4, arable land could, at a cost, be expanded considerably, if necessary.

[7] Actual U.S. per capita food intake is about 3,200 calories per day or 1.2 million calories per year while the world average food intake is 2,400 calories per day or 0.78 million calories per year. In reality, of course, it is not just calories which matter. In particular, sufficient protein in the diet is of great concern in most of the less-developed countries. However, 1.5 million calories per year would seem to be enough in excess of actual caloric needs to provide for adequate (but not generous) protein in the diet.

[8] Personal communication.

[9] C. T. De Wit, "Food Production: Past, Present, and Future," *Stikstof*, No. 15 (January 1972), pp. 68–80.

[10] Under conditions of extreme phosphorus scarcity, a diet with fewer meats and animal products (and possible substitution of "synthetic" meats now on the market) could be expected; so a population more like 8 billion than 3 billion would be possible.

[11] De Wit, "Food Production," p. 73. The major factor responsible for the difference in fresh yield weights between cereal grains and potatoes is the amount of water contained in each. Cereals contain about 10 percent water while potatoes are about 80 percent water. The way to make yields comparable is to exclude the water content and express yields in terms of organic matter. Part of the difference in yields is due to the fact that a much higher percentage of the organic matter of potato plants (80 percent) is in the edible portion than in cereal crops (50 percent). Also, the growing season for potatoes is longer so their theoretical yield is greater.

[12] Ibid., pp. 73–74. Kilocalorie (kcal), meaning kilogram calorie or large calorie, is synonymous with our term calorie.

[13] For comparison, Bradfield ("Training Agronomists," p. 60) obtained an annual yield of about 22.5 tons per hectare in his field experiments. This is about 20 tons of dry organic matter since the crops were rice and sorghum, containing little water.

[14] The effect of doubling the amount of currently arable land is considered in Chapter 5.

[15] De Wit calculates that on average 260 m² of land would be needed to supply 2 million calories per year for each person. De Wit states that another 750 m² of land per person would be needed for living and working space and for parks and natural environment. This total of 1,000 m² per person is about the density of Malta or Bermuda (according to Table 2 of the United Nations, *Demographic Yearbook, 1970*). At this density the potential world population would be 130 billion.

Based on 1,500 m² of land for living space and 260 m² for growing food, De Wit calculates the world population would be reduced to about 75 billion. This is about 5.7 persons per hectare (10,000 m² per hectare) above the existing densities of the Netherlands (3.2 persons per hectare), Japan (3.8), South Korea (3.2), Taiwan (3.9), the states of New Jersey (3.7) or Rhode Island (3.5), and well above the density of the world as it exists now (0.3). On the other hand, population densities in U.S. cities generally exceed 5.7 people per hectare (1,760 m² per person), 10 people per hectare (1,000 m² per person), and even in some cases 38.5 people per hectare (260 m² per person): Baltimore has 44.7 per hectare; Cleveland, 38.2;

Detroit, 42.3; St. Louis, 39.3; and Yonkers, 44.6. New York City has 101.7 people per hectare, and the Borough of Manhattan in that city has 261.8 residents per hectare (or only 38.2 m² per person). (Data from *Statistical Abstract of the United States—1971*.) In view of the problems associated with such dense areas, other limits might prevent such worldwide densities. As De Wit notes ("Food Production," p. 74):

A comparison of the above figures shows that the size of the world population does not depend so much on the area of the land that is needed for agricultural production, as on the land surface which is needed for other purposes, so that the supply of food is not the limiting factor. More likely the limiting factor will be mutual irritation or the impossibility of getting rid of our waste products.

[16] De Wit, "Food Production," p. 77.

[17] Vincent Sauchelli, *Phosphates in Agriculture*, 2nd ed. (New York: Reinhold Publishing Corporation, 1965), pp. 88–99.

[18] These data also suggest, however, that in many other countries phosphate reserves in the soil are being depleted. W. P. Martin, W. F. Fenster and L. D. Hanson, "Fertilizer Management for Pollution Control," in Ted L. Willrich and George E. Smith, eds., *Agricultural Practices and Water Quality* (Ames: The Iowa State University Press, 1970), pp. 143–144, cite other work showing that, in the United States, fertilizer applications of P are about equivalent to withdrawals of P in crops. With about 10 kg. of phosphorus in commercial inorganic fertilizer applied to each arable hectare in the United States, withdrawals by crops may even exceed these inputs, as typical U.S. crop yields remove about 20 kg. per hectare. See Malcolm H. McVickar, *Using Commercial Fertilizers: Commercial Fertilizers and Crop Production*, 3rd ed. (Danville, Illinois: Interstate Printers and Publishers, Inc., 1970), pp. 155–160. In addition, soil erosion losses add to the gap. The difference between applications of P fertilizer in commercial form and removal by crops is probably accounted for in part by P in rainfall, by manure, and by the return of nonedible plant remains. In the long run this "mining" of P out of the topsoil probably cannot be maintained.

[19] In a review of the first draft of this study, Dr. Carl Carlson of the Agricultural Research Service in the U.S. Department of Agriculture agreed that the 2.7 rule used by TIE for predicting phosphorus depletion is "invalid" and that a 20 kg. rule would be more "realistic." (T. C. Byerly, Office of the Secretary, U.S. Department of Agriculture, letter communication.)

4

Conservation
and Recycling

Conservation Measures and Solutions

There are, of course, reasons other than those given thus far to believe
the calculations in Tables 1 and 2 are overestimates of the amount of
phosphorus that would be used at high population levels. One is the
fact that the two formulas for projecting phosphorus use are both
based on current costs of phosphate fertilizers, whereas, if the costs of
obtaining P rose because of diminishing quality of source ore or because of other factors, much more careful use of P would be made.[1]

At its current low cost in the developed countries (relative, that is,
to costs of other inputs), farmers there do not find it profitable to
measure and distribute P fertilizer as carefully as possible, especially
since not much is known about the optimal amounts and placement of
fertilizer for the many crops, soils, and climate combinations.[2] For example, experiments indicate that the usual practice of broadcasting
phosphate fertilizer is significantly less efficient (only 40 percent as
efficient in terms of crop yields in one such experiment) than applying
it in pellet form.[3]

Certainly as the price of P began to approach the ultimate level indicated in tables 1 and 2 (or as the environmental costs rose), much
greater attention would be paid to reducing its use to the lowest possible level. Not only would P be applied in pellet form, or an even better
form yet to be discovered, but also substantial research would be undertaken to determine the optimum amounts and levels of its use.

Substitution Possibilities.   Although phosphorus is essential for plant and animal life, there may be a range over which substitutes in some sense may exist. Increased use of insect and weed killers may reduce the need for fertilizer because of decreased competition for the soil nutrients. Even increased dosages of nitrogen and potassium may offset, to a very limited extent, part of the phosphorus applied.

It is impossible to sort out such effects from the two projection formulas since they only relate total fertilizer use to crop yields. As noted earlier, this is an important deficiency because increased use of fertilizer is usually associated with increases in other inputs (irrigation water, biocides) and with improved yield practices (better seeds, soil management). It is really not possible to tell what part of the increased yields are due to increased phosphate fertilizer as opposed to other fertilizers and inputs. However, the extent of these substitution possibilities has yet to be determined for high-output situations.

The substitution of land for phosphate fertilizer could be a major avenue to reduce P consumption rates. Both the 2.7 rule and the modified FAO formula predict per hectare quantities of fertilizer, and the calculations in Tables 1 and 2 are based on a constant cultivated area of about 1,400 million ha. It has been estimated, however, that the amount of potentially arable land is over double this, or 3,200 million ha.[4]

This land area, however, represents only 24 percent of the total ice-free land surface of the earth; additional land could be added through investment—often substantial—in bringing water to deserts, protecting crops from cold temperatures, clearing land of stones and trees, and additional research on the problem. Through time, as knowledge about types of soil and climate has been increased, the estimates of potentially arable land have increased, and probably will continue to do so.[5] For example, the sandy soils of Florida and the southeastern United States were once believed to be infertile but are now quite productive.[6] On the other hand, as noted in Appendix B, the actual increase in the amount of arable land has been very small in recent years. Part of the difference between the observed, very slow increase in arable land and the increases in potentially arable land is that some potentially arable land has been urbanized or converted to other uses.

In any event, it is probably wrong to classify certain areas as being either arable or nonarable. There is no sharp division, but a gradation of acceptable soils—some areas are better than others for growing crops, but at differing levels of expense most can be made to grow crops.

While De Wit argues strongly that crops could be grown more intensively on even fewer acres than at present,[7] there may come a time when additional land must be cultivated because further increases in output would not be possible except by very large increases in fertilizer and other inputs. If, in contrast to the analysis by De Wit, the 2.7 rule and the modified FAO formula are correct, then certainly additional land could be substituted in the place of more fertilizer.

To make this more concrete, assume that the arable land is doubled. For a population of 20 billion, the density per arable hectare would be halved, and the annual usage of P fertilizer according to the 2.7 rule would be cut from 1,160 million tons (Table 1) to 360 million tons.[8] Similarly, for the modified FAO formula, a doubling of arable land would reduce annual P usage from 410 million tons (Table 2) to about 260 million tons. Since arable land could ultimately be increased beyond this level, even lower levels of phosphate fertilizer use could be obtained.

Impact of Technological Change. The two prediction formulas also fail to take future advances in technology into account. Given rising prices for phosphate fertilizer, there would be a positive stimulant to conduct research to develop crops which would need less phosphorus without sacrificing protein content. There already exist significant differences in the phosphate levels of various crops, although to some extent a lower percentage of P content is associated with lower protein content. Rice, for example, contains 0.35 percent P, while corn contains 0.45 percent.[9] Selective breeding and improved varieties might bring about further reductions in the phosphorus uptake of crops (without sacrificing their quality—i.e., protein content) and also perhaps increase the ability of crops to extract phosphorus from soils.

Numerous other research possibilities exist. As indicated above, much remains to be learned about the management of phosphate fertilizer and its uptake and utilization by plants. For the times involved here (hundreds and thousands of years) it would be impossible to predict what advances in technology might bring about in conserving phosphorus but they could be significant, even if the price of phosphate does not rise very much.

Hydroponics. There are, of course, some fairly extreme nutrient conservation measures that are within the present state of the art. Hydroponics or soilless culture is one such alternative. Hydroponic cultivation involves growing crops in closed boxes or tanks; thus, there is essentially no way for such nutrients as P, N, or K to escape in any amount except as they are incorporated into the plants themselves. This method would also eliminate any possible eutrophication or other direct pollution problems from fertilizers.[10]

However, as far as phosphorus alone is concerned, the same results could probably be achieved at much less cost by advanced soil erosion control methods, since almost all of the P reaching water bodies does so by soil erosion. Unfortunately, the same is not true of N and K, as they are substantially more soluble in water and, therefore, drain off the soil into the water table. If these problems and the relatively minor losses of P by leaching do become important enough, it is always possible to resort to hydroponics as a last (and expensive) resort.

However, not everyone agrees that food production in hydroponic greenhouses would be very expensive. Taylor and Humpstone claim that plastic greenhouses with recirculation of the irrigation water would avoid environmental problems and yet might not cost too much.[11] They state (pp. 52–53) that the plastic greenhouse capital costs are "now less than $1 per square foot of enclosed area and are expected to continue to decrease" and that "the capital costs of heating, ventilating, water equipment, etc. bring the total capital costs to between $1 and $2 per square foot for large plastic greenhouse systems now in use in the United States." They state further (p. 56) that "a currently conceivable goal for large-scale systems" might be 25 cents per square foot of enclosed area ($2.70 per square meter). By controlling temperature, humidity, carbon dioxide level, water and nutrients, they believe that about ten tons of harvest food (on a dry basis) could be grown annually on each greenhouse acre (about 25 tons per hectare). This ten tons would, they claim, support about fifteen people at the current U.S. standard (thirty-seven people per hectare). (Ten tons of harvested dry food equivalent is, at 4,000 calories per kilogram, 40 million calories or $2\frac{2}{3}$ million calories per person per year.)

For fifteen people per acre, about 3,000 ft^2 of enclosed greenhouse area would be necessary for each person (270 m^2). The per capita investment cost at 25 cents per square foot they calculate to be $750, or amortized over ten years, $75 per person per year. As for operating costs, they state (p. 56) that "direct operating costs are likely to be comparable to present costs of open-field agriculture—higher costs of heating fuel, plastic replacement, etc., being roughly balanced by much higher densities of crops and associated lower costs of harvesting."

While agreeing that the additional annual per capita costs of $75 are "well beyond the reach of any but the world's wealthiest nations, at least for many decades," (p. 56), they conclude that there is some basis for even lower costs through technology and mass markets (pp. 56–57):

The required plastic sheeting and supporting wire structures can now be made for less than two cents per square foot, and even this cost can be expected to drop further if there were a large worldwide market for the materials. It is not beyond reason that large enclosures might eventually be erected, using low-cost local labor (in the less developed nations), for only a few cents per square foot—conceivably reducing the total costs of greenhouse systems to as little as five cents per square foot.

At 5 cents instead of 25 cents per square foot, the annual additional per capita costs would be reduced from $75 to $15.

However, while these costs might be achieved in the long run, even $75 per capita per year seems too low for attainment within the existing levels of technological knowledge. Taylor and Humpstone concentrate on the cost of the plastic enclosure but may be underestimating the costs of underlining the soil or growth medium with an impermeable material (so that the irrigation water can be recirculated without significant losses) and the costs of the recirculation system and the environmental control system. That is, the present costs of one or two dollars per square foot cited by Taylor and Humpstone may be figures for constructing average types of plastic greenhouses but the "average" plastic greenhouse does not involve as much environmental control (and particularly does not involve total collection and recirculation of the irrigation water) as would be needed to avoid escape of the plant nutrients. Dana Dalrymple of the U.S. Department of Agriculture states that "many of these hydroponic greenhouses have been commercially manufactured," and that some plastic units "with virtually complete environmental equipment" cost about $18,200 per 3,300 square foot unit when erected in the United States in early 1972.[12] At $5.50 per square foot (about $59 per square meter), the capital cost of 3,000 ft² per person would be $16,500—a long way from the Taylor and Humpstone estimate of $750. Based on a ten-year amortization period, annual per capita costs of the hydroponic enclosure would be $1,650, but a more realistic annual fixed charge rate would be 20 percent rather than 10 percent so the annual costs would be $3,300 per capita. While mass production would greatly reduce these costs, it is not clear that within the existing state of technology annual per capita costs would be reduced to $75.

In addition, Dalrymple indicates, the costs of operating average (nonhydroponic) greenhouses are quite high, primarily because of costs for heating and labor. For example, in the mid-1960s Dalrymple shows that operating costs in U.S. greenhouses were about 60 cents per square foot of $1,800 for the 3,000 ft² necessary for each person (Dalrymple, p. 65). However, these costs are not entirely reasonable since they consist of the costs for raising tomatoes, which are more labor intensive than most crops. A somewhat more appropriate (but not perfect) comparison is between the costs of nongreenhouse (field) tomatoes and greenhouse tomatoes. From data compiled by Dalrymple (pp. 66–69 and 77–79), the Midwest wholesale delivered price of greenhouse tomatoes was about two or three times higher than the wholesale delivered price of field tomatoes, but usually the field tomatoes were shipped a much longer distance than the greenhouse tomatoes (from Florida, California or Mexico to the Midwest versus local Midwest greenhouse production) so this comparison understates the cost difference. To some extent, the better quality of greenhouse tomatoes offsets this shipping distance factor but the production costs of greenhouse tomatoes may still be as much as five times as great as those of field tomatoes. (It should be noted that greenhouse tomatoes can compete with lower-priced field tomatoes not only because of quality differences but primarily because greenhouse tomatoes are brought to market at times when field tomatoes are not available.)

It is unclear whether the same sort of cost differential would apply to grain and other crops but certainly there would be an increase of some magnitude. If operating expenses in the United States in 1972 increased by a factor of five for all farm production, then these costs would rise from $35 billion to $175 billion, or from $170 per person to $840 per person.[13] This increase of $670 per capita in operating expenses plus the annualized capital costs of $3,300 would certainly be an impossible burden at this time. Even if these figures are overestimates by a large amount, it is still clear that hydroponic farming is likely to impose too great a cost. Nevertheless, improvements in technology—especially in the direction of automation of labor-intensive tasks—plus the general increase in per capita productivity and income over time eventually might well bring about the sorts of results which Taylor and Humpstone envisage.

An Ultimate Solution. Although the day of significant phosphorus scarcity appears quite far off, the ultimate solution would be the replacement of the crop cycle. In its place, food could be synthesized from coal, oil, limestone, or other carbon substances to produce the necessary carbohydrate calories for humans.[14] The essential amino acids for human protein needs have already been synthesized and used to supplement protein-poor diets in underdeveloped countries. Vitamins are also routinely synthesized throughout the world. Fats were synthesized on a small scale during World War II in Germany. Thus, the technology already exists to bypass the conventional crop cycle.

In this event, the only phosphate necessary would be about 1 gm. of P a day per person since crops would not be needed.[15] Allowing for losses of 50 percent, 2 gm. of P per day would total to 0.7 kg. per year. Under these conditions, phosphate deposits would last millions of years.

Recycling

Up to this point only brief reference has been made to the recycling of phosphorus. The use of manure and composted nonedible plant residues has been discussed and is the most obvious and traditional form of recycling. In a certain sense reduction of soil erosion losses of P (discussed above and in Appendix D) is also recycling, since the P not lost from the soil is being returned to, or kept in, the soil. However, most of the analysis above and the resulting estimates of exhaustion periods have been related to mining of P and its use on a once-through basis.

Implicit in most of these calculations is the assumption that approximately the same percentage level of recycling of P as now practiced (through use of manure and plant residues as fertilizer) would continue into the future. Increasing the percentage of P recycled can, of course, greatly extend the calculated exhaustion periods. It may also be a much less expensive alternative than mining P from common rocks, or resorting to hydroponics and food manufactured from coal or limestone.

Agricultural Recycling. It is obvious that nearly all the P used is not lost from the earth but merely returned, often in very dilute form, into streams and rivers and eventually into lakes and oceans. As indicated, most of the P lost from fertilizer applications is in runoff and soil erosion or in the crops themselves. Very little P is lost by leaching or other routes. If leaching losses did prove significant, underlining of soils by asphaltic or plastic substances could be used to reduce these losses of P (and soil moisture). Such a system would resemble hydroponic farming, a rather expensive solution to this problem.

Preventing losses of P by controlling soil erosion and water runoff is not exactly recycling but may be much cheaper than attempting to extract P out of very dilute sources such as rivers and streams. The rough order-of-magnitude costs developed in Appendix D, under possibly favorable conditions, are about $500 per metric ton of P retained in the soil, but soil erosion and runoff control have other associated benefits in maintaining the topsoil and eliminating pollutants in the aquatic environment.

Crops contain significant amounts of P, with perhaps 20 or 30 kg. of P in a single crop grown on one hectare.[16] Portions of the crop which are often left on the soil (roots, straw, stems, etc.—the plant residues) contain roughly one-third of this amount. If these nonedible (by humans) plant residues are plowed into the soil, the contained P would then be transferred mostly to succeeding crops. However, plowing may increase soil erosion (and the loss of P in the soil): directly, by loosening the soil; and indirectly, by removing the protective shield of the plant residues. On the other hand, as Aldrich et al. point out,[17] not plowing residues under in a no-plow tillage system of farming may lead to loss of the P from the plant residues themselves.

If these portions not edible by humans are fed to animals, the manures can be recycled to the soil as fertilizer. Use of manure in this way has the added advantage of reducing surface water runoff and the loss of phosphorus.[18] The economics of manure versus inorganic commercial fertilizer does not currently favor careful collection and use of manure in the more developed countries (because of the low percentage of P and other nutrients per ton of manure),[19] but it is clear that this traditional source of P is far cheaper than the estimated ultimate costs of P from common rock. At the same time, the disposal of manure, especially from animal feedlots, has become a pollution problem which would be largely eliminated if the price of P were to rise high enough to induce its use once more as a fertilizer.

The small proportion of phosphate intake not excreted by animals remains in their bodies. About 80 percent of the body phosphorus is contained in their bones. Thus, dried, ground bones, with about 10 percent P content, were once an important source of fertilizer and are still used as animal feed supplements. A large percentage of the P incorporated into the bodies of animals could be recycled at a relatively low cost.

Sewage Recycling.　　Similar comments apply to the crops eaten by humans. In certain poor countries much of the P is recycled through the use of human waste ("night-soil") as fertilizer. It is also at least possible, if not very appealing, to use human bones as sources of phosphorus. The removal of P from sewage systems has also been investigated and a fairly high level of recovery is possible.[20]

Assuming an average level of 10 parts per million P in the sewage, a 90 percent recovery of the P, and a cost of 3 to 5 cents per 1,000 gallons of effluent,[21] the cost of P recovered ranges between $900 and $1,500 per metric ton.[22] Although the P must be further processed before it can be made into fertilizer, this step is apparently not very expensive and is often undertaken in order to recover the calcium used to precipitate the P out of sewage.[23]

Weinberger states that commercial firms now claim this removal of P can be achieved at 2 cents per 1,000 gallons ($600 per metric ton of P). There are also efforts to reduce these costs and increase the recovery of P to above 95 percent.[24] Again, such removal processes may be widely adopted in developed countries because of potential pollution problems, quite apart from the value of phosphorus.

Removal of P from sewage, and for that matter, from industrial waste water, obviously catches the phosphate used in detergents and other nonfertilizer nonfood applications as well. However, because of the possible role such sources of P have in accelerating the rate of eutrophication, restrictions may greatly reduce these nonfertilizer uses. If P were to become more scarce, with an accompanying price rise, substitutes would be found for most of these applications in any event.[25]

It is also possible to bypass extracting P from sewage by applying the sewage directly on the soil as fertilizer. This practice has been carried out with very beneficial effects for many years in some areas but the lower costs of commercial fertilizers (and the introduction of toxic substances into sewage flows) have tended to greatly restrict its use in this manner.[26] The cost of recycling P in this manner is probably much less (in terms of dollars per ton of P applied as fertilizer) than the current cost of extracting P from sewage.[27]

Other Sources of Recovery. Before the inorganic fertilizer industry existed, bird guano, fish scraps, and other organic wastes were an important source of fertilizer. These organic sources are little used now but, if scarcity approached, could be. Another source is ground basic slag, still an important source of phosphate fertilizer in Europe where high-grade phosphorus ore deposits are scarce. Basic slag, containing roughly 3 to 8 percent P, is a by-product of steel plants using phosphatic iron ores in the basic Bessemer or basic open-hearth processes, both of which are now obsolete.[28]

Finally, there remains the possibility of recycling phosphate from lake beds and the ocean floor. Since the sea floor is the ultimate depository for phosphorus,[29] it may eventually be cheaper to remove the concentrations of P off the sea floor (and lake bottoms) than to resort to mining common rocks.

It has already been mentioned that certain phosphate deposits on the continental sea floor have been considered for their economic potential, and, at the significantly higher costs which may have to be encountered some day, further exploitation of this source may be reasonable. Such sea mining would then close the recycling loop.

Recycling Conclusions. The above comments on recycling are obviously only suggestions. While the discussion is not definitive, it certainly does tend to show that much of the P consumed can be reused. There is not enough information available to determine exactly what percentage at what cost but it is probably a fairly high percentage at costs not greatly in excess of existing costs of P.

Given that a good portion of the P taken out of the soil by crops can be (and is, in less-developed countries) returned quite cheaply in the form of manure or composted plant residues, it is difficult to agree to the statement that "phosphorus is essentially a nonrenewable resource."[30] It is true that the other major, long-run dissipative loss of phosphate—in soil erosion and runoff—is more expensive to prevent but it seems clear that, before phosphorus is extracted from granite at $11,000 per ton, it would pay to recycle a very high percentage of P, especially if environmental damages rise in proportion to use.

Notes

[1] Costs of phosphate fertilizer could rise even if the ore grade for P did not decline because ore deposits might be further from markets, smaller in size, further underground, more difficult to beneficiate, etc. In addition, fertilizers are subsidized to encourage their use in some countries; elimination of these subsidies would increase the price and decrease the use of fertilizer. To the extent the environmental

costs of phosphate fertilizer manufacture and usage are paid for by, or are passed along to, farmers, the price of phosphate fertilizer will also increase and similarly encourage conservation.

[2] See S. R. Aldrich, W. R. Oschwald, and J. B. Fehrenbacher, "Implications of Crop-Production Technology for Environmental Quality," in *Land Use Problems in Illinois*, arranged by Robert E. Bergstrom, Environmental Geology Notes of the Illinois State Geological Survey, No. 46 (May 1971). They claim that: "Phosphorus applications have been raised to unrealistically high levels in many Illinois fields. . . . It appears that many farmers either did not know what their tests [for P] were or were unfamiliar with agronomic research showing that they had exceeded the most profitable point. . . . Phosphorus fertilizer applications in the future can be reduced on many fields, though it should be increased on others," (pp. 13–14). Similar conclusions are reached in *Agricultural Pollution of the Great Lakes Basin*, combined report by Canada and the United States for the U.S. Environmental Protection Agency (Washington, D.C.: Government Printing Office, July 1, 1971), pp. 16–20, 30 of Part B.

[3] FAO, *Statistics of Crop Responses to Fertilizers* (Rome: FAO, 1966), pp. 17–20.

[4] President's Science Advisory Committee, Panel on the World Food Supply, *The World Food Problem*. (Washington, D.C.: Government Printing Office, 1967), vol. II, pp. 427–428. Development of these additional 1,800 million ha. would involve varying amounts of investment.

[5] Charles E. Kellogg and Arnold C. Orvedal, "Potentially Arable Soils of the World and Critical Measures for Their Use," *Advances in Agronomy*, vol. 21 (1969), pp. 140–141. Kellogg and Orvedal state, "As agricultural research continues, doubtless these estimates will appear low to soil scientists of the year 2000."

[6] PSAC, vol. II, pp. 409–410.

[7] C. T. De Wit, "Food Production: Past, Present, and Future," *Stikstof*, No. 15 (January 1972), pp. 68–80.

[8] The 360 million ton estimate was calculated by solving for the rate of use by a population of 10 billion and then doubling the answer. That is, the rate of usage was calculated for a population of 10 billion in the same manner as in Table 1: $Z = (11.3) \cdot (N/3.6)^{2.7}$, where Z is the annual use of P in fertilizer in millions of tons per year and N is the world population in billions. For $N = 10$, $Z = 178.3$. However, this covers only half the population so the answer must be doubled. A similar procedure was used for the FAO estimating equation as employed in the calculations for Table 2.

[9] Vincent Sauchelli, *Phosphates in Agriculture*, 2nd ed. (New York: Reinhold Publishing Corporation, 1965), p. 89. The percentages relate to rice and corn on a dry basis. It should be noted, however, that the protein content of corn is superior to that of rice.

[10] The role of phosphate, and particularly phosphate fertilizer, in bringing about increased rates of eutrophication is currently a subject of great debate.

[11] Theodore B. Taylor and Charles C. Humpstone, *The Restoration of the Earth* (New York: Harper & Row, 1973), pp. 52–58. They argue that total containment of all man-made pollutants is not only desirable but feasible.

[12] Dana G. Dalrymple, *Controlled Environmental Agriculture: A Global Review of Greenhouse Food Production*, Economic Research Service of the U.S. Department of Agriculture, Foreign Agricultural Economic Report No. 89, October 1973 (Washington, D.C.: Government Printing Office, 1973), p. 32.

[13] From data in *Statistical Abstract of the United States*, 1973, pp. 5 and 595.

[14] N. W. Pirie, *Food Resources: Conventional and Novel* (Baltimore: Penguin Books, 1969), pp. 158–159.

¹⁵ Some crops could be grown with their P requirements drawn from soil reserves and organic sources.

¹⁶ Malcolm H. McVickar, *Using Commercial Fertilizers: Commercial Fertilizers and Crop Production*, pp. 155–160.

¹⁷ Aldrich et al., "Implications of Crop-Production Technology," p. 15.

¹⁸ Cornell University, Department of Agronomy, College of Agricultural and Life Sciences, *Management of Nutrients on Agricultural Land for Improved Quality* (Ithaca, N.Y.: Cornell University Press, August 1971), p. 3.

¹⁹ Sauchelli, *Phosphates in Agriculture*, pp. 192–193.

²⁰ The TIE report dismisses such recycling as follows: "Urbanization and sewerage systems concentrate wastes so that they can be treated, but even with secondary treatment about 70% of the phosphorus passes through into the effluent." (TIE report, p. 51). Systems and methods to specifically remove phosphorus from secondary effluent are not discussed.

²¹ Leon W. Weinberger, "Waste Treatment for Phosphorus Removal," statement at the Lake Michigan Enforcement Conference, February 1, 1968, reprinted in U.S. Senate, Committee on Public Works, *Water Pollution—1970*, Hearings Before the Subcommittee on Air and Water Pollution, 91st Congress, 2nd Session, 1970, pp. 1555–1565. Robert Smith and Richard G. Eilers, *Cost to the Consumer for Collection and Treatment of Wastewater*, for the U.S. Environmental Protection Agency (Washington, D.C.: Government Printing Office, July 1970), pp. 12, 14, 15, 34, 38, and 39.

²² At 10 parts per million, 1,000 gallons of effluent water (which weighs 3,782 kg.) contains 0.0378 kg. of P. Of this, 90 percent, or 0.034038 kg. of P, is recovered.

²³ Weinberger, "Waste Treatment for Phosphorus Removal," pp. 1558–1559.

²⁴ Gilbert V. Levin et al., "Pilot-Plant Tests of a Phosphate Removal Process," *Journal, Water Pollution Control Federation*, Vol. 44, No. 10 (1972), pp. 1940–1953; and R. L. Hummell and J. W. Smith, "Profitable Phosphate Recovery from Secondary Sewage Waste Effluent by Reciprocating Flow Ion Exchange," in U.S. Senate Committee on Public Works, *Water Pollution—1970*, pp. 1930–1949. The process proposed by Hummell and Smith would allow over 99 percent removal of P, at a profit through sale of the phosphorus.

²⁵ This does raise the interesting question of what happens to the costs of extracting P from sewage as less P is used. The more dilute the P concentration is in sewage, the higher the cost (per ton of P) of removing it. Direct processing of P from concentrated sources (such as organic wastes) could be applied before these wastes were released into sewage streams. However, the general principle that rising scarcity and increased costs of P will reduce its use and therefore raise the price of extracting it from disposal media also applies to other measures, such as erosion control.

²⁶ Vladimir Ignatieff and Harold J. Page, eds., *Efficient Use of Fertilizers* (revised ed.), FAO Agricultural Studies No. 43 (Rome: FAO, 1958), pp. 42–49; and R. R. Parizek et al., *Waste Water Renovation and Conservation*, The Pennsylvania State University Studies No. 23 (University Park, Pennsylvania, 1967), reprinted in U.S. Senate, Committee on Public Works, *Water Pollution–1970*, pp. 1011–1079. (Also associated materials on pp. 988–1010.)

²⁷ Since much of the phosphate in sewage and wastes is evidently in an "unavailable" or insoluble form that makes it more difficult for plants to absorb it, processing of these phosphate sources into more available fertilizer forms might be necessary. This can apparently be accomplished in much the same way fertilizers are made out of phosphate rock today. Toxic substances could be collected separately so they would not enter the sewer system.

²⁸ Sauchelli, *Phosphates in Agriculture*, pp. 147–149.
²⁹ According to the TIE report, p. 50, "The natural movement of phosphorus is slow. Phosphates which are leached (in dissolved form) or eroded (in particulate form) from the land find their way to streams and lakes. Some of them are precipitated in lake sediments, but the rest enter the ocean where they, too, are precipitated.

As the bodies of animals and plants that have accumulated phosphorus fall to lower levels, surface waters of the oceans become depleted of phosphate supplies. But, deep water tends to be nearly saturated (calcium is abundant), so that the additions from above are precipitated to the sediment. Upswelling of deep water returns some phosphorus to the surface, but this amount is always limited by the relative insolubility of calcium phosphate."
³⁰ Ibid., p. 50.

5
Summary and Concluding Observations

The object of this study has been to examine the TIE thesis that "Known potential supplies of phosphorus, a nonrenewable resource essential to life, will be exhausted before the end of the 21st century."[1] The analysis conducted in this study indicates that the TIE report conclusions are wrong, and that calculated exhaustion times are more on the order of thousands or millions of years. To support our contention, both supply and demand side estimates are considered.

Deposits

A major factor which originally led to the TIE conclusion was its calculated upper limit of "usable" phosphorus deposits of 30 billion metric tons. This figure was found to have been in error and should have been 30 trillion, but this included unknown as well as known deposits. G. D. Emigh, an expert in the field, estimated that there are about 180 billion tons of P in known deposits, consisting of current or commercial grade deposits of 20 billion tons, and somewhat submarginal, but still usable, deposits of 160 billion tons in specific known locations. Although it is possible to overestimate the quantities of P in these various deposits, the opposite appears to be true: Emigh left several known deposits out of his summation because not enough was known about the quantities involved, and he consistently underestimated the reserve quantities for those deposits included. In certain instances it may turn out that his estimates for particular deposits were too large but overall it is highly unlikely reserves will be less than his total estimate.

The more important point in comparing the TIE estimate of the theoretical upper limit of usable P with the Emigh estimate of known deposits is the question of what is "usable." Some of the deposits in Emigh's calculation include phosphorus from ores with less than 8 percent P, but according to the TIE report, 8 percent P is the lower limit of "potentially usable" ore. However, as Emigh points out, restricting attention to ores containing only 8 percent P or more has no logical or factual basis.[2] At a given, fixed level of technology, all that happens as lower grades are used is that the costs of extraction increase. In addition, in the past at least, improvements in technology through time have offset, or more than offset—for a wide variety of natural resources—the costs of going to leaner and leaner ore sources.[3]

In this connection, ideally, one might want to trace out the costs, with today's technology, of extracting and beneficiating phosphorus to a level acceptable for processing into fertilizer for all grades of phosphorus ore. Unfortunately, although phosphate ore specialists (e.g., Emigh and the U.S. Geological Survey experts) agree that there are vast quantities of lower-grade P ores available, no quantitative estimates of the amounts are available. However, cost and quantity information on phosphorus in common rock is available. Thus, leaving out all sources between an average of 8 percent phosphate ore and common rock (about 0.1 percent P), it was estimated that there are about 600 trillion tons of recoverable P under the top two miles of ground covering the continents (excluding Antarctica).

The cost of extracting and beneficiating the P out of this source with existing technology was roughly estimated by a researcher at Oak Ridge National Laboratory (ORNL) to be about 200 times 1972 costs, or on the order of $10,000 per metric ton. Since this cost figure includes nothing for the possibly serious environmental damages from mining, another $1,000 per ton was added to cover restoration costs. The environmental costs of $1,000 per ton of P would total $42 million per hectare—a huge sum by present standards but perhaps not in terms of the large-scale mining envisioned in removing P from common rock.

It hardly requires mentioning that the expansion from 20 or 180 billion tons of P to 600 trillion tons (again, leaving out the huge amounts of lower intermediate grade P ore) *greatly* extends calculated exhaustion periods. The more serious question then becomes per capita cost rather than exhaustion time.

Phosphorus Fertilizer Consumption Estimates

It is legitimate to ask, given the deposit estimates discussed above, what value further examination of this situation has. While the time of phosphorus exhaustion is probably thousands or millions of years off, the TIE consumption formula is worth examining since it is of the type commonly used in similar studies of resource availability over time. Whatever light can be shed here on the general question of projecting very long-run consumption levels may, therefore, be of value for future studies of this type.

Attention has been focused almost exclusively on the use of phosphorus in fertilizers. This was done because probably over 80 percent of all P is used in fertilizer applications. This percentage is likely to increase if phosphorus becomes more scarce since most nonfertilizer uses of P have ready substitutes. The possible (but hotly debated) environmental consequences of P in detergents and industrial applications causing eutrophication may bring about reduction in these areas of use in any event. Also, the projected consumption rates are based on total production, not production merely for fertilizer usage. Therefore, all existing nonfertilizer uses of P are treated as if they were used for fertilizer.

The consumption projection relation used in the TIE report links it with population size. Under the assumptions that per capita crop output and the amount of arable land do not increase, the relationship states that commercial inorganic phosphorus fertilizer use must increase 2.7 times as fast as the population.[4] The derivation of this 2.7 rule is haphazard in the extreme—it is based on aggregates for three countries for three years, a total of nine data points. The underlying regression relates agricultural crop output per hectare to fertilizer per hectare at the expense of ignoring all other inputs.

Amazingly enough, the 2.7 rule, over a limited range of output increases, gives results very close to those of a prediction equation more carefully derived by FAO researchers and revised for use in the President's Science Advisory Committee study. Although the aggregate per hectare output and fertilizer use for many more countries are used in the FAO regression, again only fertilizer input is used to explain crop output.

However, for population increases beyond about 10 billion, the 2.7 rule projects much higher per capita or per hectare fertilizer consumption levels than the FAO equation, and the latter is much more in line with what considerations of the physical phosphorus requirements for crop growth indicate for large population sizes. In fairness to their originators, however, neither the 2.7 rule nor the FAO formula were intended for the kind of extrapolations used in the TIE study. They were both derived to determine how much fertilizer might be used in the less-developed countries if they followed the path of the more-developed countries, and not for extrapolative projections.

Even if a very careful multiple regression had been carried out, it is unlikely that the resulting equation would be useful in long-run predictions. For one thing, the range of current phosphate prices is not likely to indicate what will happen under more severe scarcity conditions. At much higher prices, phosphate fertilizer would be applied more carefully and other inputs would be substituted to the extent possible. While the necessary experiments could be carried out to determine these possibilities within the existing level of technology, such experimental results in a useful form could not be found.

More importantly, the multiple regression approach ignores the underlying physical processes. If population and crop production were to stop increasing immediately, the amount of P applied in fertilizer would probably have to increase over the long run because in many areas the P removed by crops and soil erosion exceeds that added by fertilizer. In some areas in developed countries the reverse is true—more P has been added than removed—but overall there has been a net "mining" of P out of the topsoil. It can be seen from this that the stock of P in the soil is just as important as its flow into the soil, but the regression approach tends to look only at the latter.

Based on the simple physical facts of how much phosphorus is contained in plant matter and how much plant matter is necessary to support a person, either directly or through animal feed, at a fairly high standard of living, it was estimated that about 10 or 20 kg. of P per capita per year would be adequate. It is true that this simple 10-to-20-kg. rule ignores the law of diminishing returns, but it is likely to provide a better long-run estimate than extrapolation of current trends. Further, the physical analysis of plant growth by De Wit and others indicates that diminishing returns for high output, long-run situations may not play a very large role—that is, the amount of choice in the quantity of P fertilizer applications may be quite limited over the long run.

The 10-to-20-kg. rule does depend upon minimizing losses other than those in crops. Since P becomes strongly fixed to (clay) soil, leaching losses are evidently insignificant. Soil erosion and runoff are the major sources of P lost but methods exist to reduce these losses to very low levels. Phosphorus fixed in the soil may also be lost in the sense that it becomes unavailable to the plants for their growth. There is uncertainty over this issue but it appears that such fixed phosphorus does become available to plants over a period of years so that it is not permanently lost. In addition, forms and methods of application and control of soil acidity can be used to increase availability. The 10-to-20-kg. estimate, in fact, can be interpreted as 5 or 10 kg. of P taken up in plants and 5 or 10 kg. of losses per year per capita.

Recycling and Other Solutions. One, rather expensive, way to ensure minimal noncrop losses of P (and other nutrients) is to grow crops in tanks as in hydroponic farming. A cheaper solution would be to increase recycling as scarcity approaches and the price increases. For example, if P must be extracted from common rock at $11,000 per ton, one can be sure that the recycling of P from manure, composted non-edible plant residues, bones and other organic waste, and industrial and urban sewage will reach very high levels—as high as or higher than once reached before chemical fertilizers were introduced.

In general, such recycling does not require much processing—the manures and wastes (except perhaps industrial wastes containing substances harmful to plants) can be applied directly or reprocessed into fertilizer and then applied. Thus, the costs are mainly those of transporting, handling, and conversion into fertilizer form. Currently in developed nations, these costs of transporting and handling of recycled materials, even those of manure already on the farm, exceed the cost of buying and applying more concentrated fertilizers.

Although a fairly high average cost was attached to recycled phosphorus at an 80 percent recycle rate ($500 per metric ton), this is probably very excessive. An 80 percent recycle level might easily be achieved at much lower costs or, at $500 per ton, a much higher percentage might be recycled. In part this estimated high cost is intended to cover reduction of soil erosion losses as well.

A final extreme solution considered was that of synthesizing food from coal, limestone, and other noncrop sources. This would allow direct feeding of phosphorus to humans. Each person requires about 1 gm. a day, so even with 50 percent losses included, the yearly per capita consumption would only be about 0.7 kg. of P.

Summary of Alternative Calculations

Table 4 summarizes the exhaustion times and costs under the various consumption assumptions discussed in this report. For simplicity, exhaustion periods and per capita costs have been shown for a constant 20 billion population. Calculations for other constant population sizes appear in Appendix A (Tables A-1, A-2, and A-3) along with a more detailed explanation of the assumptions and calculations. Probably the greatest limitation of these tables is that the average costs of P are incomplete. They do not include transport costs to the fertilizer plant or processing costs for conversion into fertilizer. Nor do these costs include the cost of land preparation in the case of doubling the amount of arable land, or for synthesizing food under the 0.7 kg. per capita direct utilization route.

In addition to the base cases reflecting the 2.7 rule and the modified FAO projection formula, the effects of an additional 80 percent recycling and doubling the cultivated land are also analyzed singly and

TABLE 4. Exhaustion Times and Per Capita Costs Under Various Alternative Phosphorus Fertilizer Consumption Assumptions (for a Constant-Size World Population of 20 Billion)

| | Net annual use (million tons) (1) | Net annual per capita use (kg.) (Col. 1 ÷ 20 bill.) (2) | Exhaustion periods recoverable | |
| | | | 20 billion tons (3) | 180 billion tons (4) |
Projection formula[a]				
2.7 rule				
1. Base case	1,160.0	57.9	17	155
2. 80% recycle	232.0	11.6	86	777
3. 2X land	357.0	17.8	56	505
4. 80% recycle, 2X land	71.0	3.6	280	2,520
FAO formula				
5. Base case	412.0	20.6	49	437
6. 80% recycle	82.0	4.1	243	2,190
7. 2X land	262.0	13.1	76	688
8. 80% recycle, 2X land	52.0	2.6	382	3,440
20 kg. per capita				
9. Base case	400.0	20.0	50	450
10. 80% recycle	80.0	4.0	250	2,250
10 kg. per capita				
11. Base case	200.0	10.0	100	900
12. 80% recycle	40.0	2.0	500	4,500
0.7 kg. per capita				
13. Base case	14.0	0.7	1,430	12,900
14. 80% recycle	2.8	0.14	7,140	64,300

[a] 2X land indicates a doubling of arable land.

[b] Exhaustion periods are calculated by dividing the indicated deposit quantity by the corresponding net annual use in Column 1. (For Column 3: 20×10^9 ÷ Column 1; for Column 4: 180×10^9 ÷ Column 1; for Column 5: 30×10^{12} ÷ Column 1; for Column 6: 590×10^{12} ÷ Column 1.)

in combination for each of these rules (rows 1 through 8). The 10 and 20 kg. per capita per year projection formulas, alternatives to the 2.7 and FAO formulas, are also analyzed alone, and with 80 percent recycling (rows 9 through 12). The 0.7 kg. of P per capita per year formula, based on eliminating the crop cycle, and on substituting food synthesis and direct ingestion of P, is utilized in rows 13 and 14.

			Annual per capita cost[c]		
30 trillion tons (5)	590 trillion tons (6)	Assumed cost ($/ton) (7)	Annual per capita cost (Col. 2 × Col. 7 ÷ 10^3) (8)	Assumed cost ($/ton) (9)	Annual per capita cost (Col. 2 × Col. 9 ÷ 10^3) (10)
25,900	509,000	$ 50	$ 2.90	$11,000	$637.00
129,000	2,550,000	2,000	23.20	13,000	151.00
84,100	1,650,000	50	0.89	11,000	196.00
421,000	8,270,000	2,000	7.20	13,000	46.80
72,800	1,430,000	50	1.03	11,000	227.00
364,000	7,160,000	2,000	8.20	13,000	53.30
115,000	2,260,000	50	0.66	11,000	144.00
573,000	11,300,000	2,000	5.20	13,000	33.80
75,000	1,475,000	50	1.00	11,000	220.00
375,000	7,375,000	2,000	8.00	13,000	52.00
150,000	2,950,000	50	0.50	11,000	110.00
750,000	14,750,000	2,000	4.00	13,000	26.00
2,140,000	42,100,000	50	0.04	11,000	7.70
10,700,000	211,000,000	2,000	0.28	13,000	1.82

[c] Costs in columns 7 and 8 should be associated with the deposit quantities indicated in columns 3–5; costs in columns 9 and 10 should be associated with deposit quantities in Column 6. All costs are partial; see text and the final section of Appendix A.

Given the assumption that recycling cuts net consumption of virgin P by a factor of five, exhaustion periods are extended by a factor of five. Thus, the effect of recycling is substantial in all cases. Doubling the amount of land has a somewhat less, but still significant, impact on exhaustion times for the 2.7 rule predictions. Doubling land for the FAO equation predictions has only a marginal impact. Substitution of the 10 kg. rule leads to sharply reduced usage rates in comparison with the 2.7 rule, but results in usage rates only 50 percent smaller than the FAO formula predictions. Synthesized food and direct consumption of 0.7 kg. P per year by humans reduces use and extends run-out times by a factor of 14 in comparison with the 10 kg. rule.

Under our assumed costs, recycling looks much more desirable than mining common rock at $11,000 per ton of P.[5] For example, from the FAO formula (line 5) 21 kg. per capita would total about $230 at $11 per kilogram. Recycling at an 80 percent level (line 6) would reduce this to about $50 (4.1 kg. times $13 per kilogram).[6] Doubling the amount of cultivated land would yield an annual cost of $140 (13 kg. times $11 per kilogram) without additional recycling (line 7) and $30 (2.6 kg. times $13 per kilogram) (line 8) with recycling. But again it must be recalled that these are partial costs only as they do not include land preparation expenditures. In addition, our assumed costs are probably not very accurate.

From such crude estimates it is possible to examine the limits of the per capita costs. The per capita costs should be bearable in developed countries. This would hold as well for the common rock case. Even in the absence of technological change which significantly reduces the cost of P from common rocks, recycling would be greatly increased as the ore grade level declined toward the lithospheric background (common rock) level. It appears that recourse to the argument that technological change will reduce the costs of extracted P from common rock is really not necessary since recycling within the present state of the art reduces the per capita costs to a bearable level, given the time horizon involved.

Results and Their Implications

Recalibration of the "reserve" of P to Emigh's totals or to common rock sources, and revision of the per capita annual requirements of P to 10 to 20 kg., leads to run-out periods on the order of a thousand to several million years. Recycling and the use of the vast quantities of intermediate grades of phosphate ore (not included in our calculations) are likely to put off the necessity to mine P out of common rock for a very long time. Furthermore, even at per ton costs deliberately estimated on the high side, annual per capita costs of P (mined and beneficiated out of common rock) are unlikely to exceed $50 because of recycling.

Under these conditions, the concept of "exhaustion" of phosphorus is incorrect. Phosphorus, except for minute amounts, does not leave the earth; it gets put into streams and other diluting environments, and the problem is the increased expense of extraction. Thus, the appropriate way to think of the running-out problem is not to say we have run out of P, but that the costs have increased. Whether this cost would ever become prohibitive is unclear, but the problem would evidently not arise for millions of years. It would perhaps depend upon whether removing P from its "final" (excluding long-run movements of the earth's crust) resting place on the bottom of the oceans would be prohibitive. There are already suggestions (e.g., deep-sea manganese nodule mining) that this source could be tapped even with today's technology.

Although actions to increase the conservation of phosphorus might be justified if it were known that its cost would become prohibitive at some distant future date, uncertainty plus the possibilities of various solutions left open to future generations—such as reducing the population over several centuries—undermine their rationale.

While some of the proposals put forward in the TIE report might be desirable on environmental grounds, it does not appear that the scarcity or running-out factor is very important. Instead attention should be directed at the current environmental aspects of phosphorus use as well as at the role of phosphate fertilizer in helping less-developed nations.

Notes

[1] The Institute of Ecology, *Man in the Living Environment*, revised edition (Madison: University of Wisconsin Press, 1972), p. 42.

[2] This approach is the source of serious error for many kindred studies as well. For example, in Donella H. Meadows et al., *The Limits to Growth* (New York: Universe Books, 1972), pp. 54–67 and 122–128; and "A Blueprint for Survival,"

The Ecologist, vol. 2, no.1 (January 1972), pp. 4, 7, and 41–42, resource exhaustion times for a variety of metals are shown but only include the estimates of commercial grade deposits such as those of the U.S. Bureau of Mines. These deposits generally encompass only slightly submarginal ores (in the case of phosphorus ores, this would be down to an average of about 8 percent P only). Meadows et al. do allow the quantity of reserves to quintuple for illustrative effect but, in view of the difference between the currently economic commercial grade deposits with 20 billion tons of P and Emigh's estimate of 180 billion tons of P or common rock deposits with about 600 trillion tons of P, much greater multiples may be involved.

Limits to Growth is also relevant since agricultural output is linked to fertilizer consumption by means of the 2.7 rule. See Dennis L. Meadows et al., *Dynamics of Growth in a Finite World* (Cambridge, Mass.: Wright–Allen Press, 1974), pp. 301–306.

[3] Harold J. Barnett and Chandler Morse, *Scarcity and Growth: The Economics of Natural Resource Availability* (Baltimore: The Johns Hopkins University Press, 1963). The conclusions of Barnett and Morse have been reaffirmed with more recent data in an as yet unpublished study under Robert Manthy of Michigan State University, sponsored by Resources for the Future, Inc. Recent events in the energy field do not disprove the Barnett–Morse conclusions—instead, those price rises are more a credit to monopoly power of the oil exporting nations than to any real resource scarcity. This is not to say that this trend will continue into the future, however. Indeed, many dispute the Barnett–Morse thesis and feel we are now at the turning point where the relative prices of minerals and other raw materials, specifically fuels, are going to rise rapidly over the long run.

[4] Thus, the use of fertilizer grows at an exponential rate. Relating the growth of fertilizer use to the population is at least superior to assuming simply (as is often done in these situations) that fertilizer use just grows forever at an exponential rate without any reference to population or output growth.

[5] The costs per ton of *net* annual use for 80 percent recycling cases in Table 4 have been derived by averaging the cost of 4 tons of recycled phosphorus with 1 ton of virgin phosphorus. The price of recycled P is assumed to be $500 per ton. The price of virgin P is assumed to be $50 per ton for Column 7 and $11,000 per ton for Column 9. For Column 7, then, 1 net ton of use represents 5 gross tons—4 tons recycled at $500 each plus 1 ton at $50, or $2,050 (rounded to $2,000). For Column 9, 1 net ton represents $13,000—4 tons at $500 each plus 1 ton at $11,000.

[6] Assuming these costs of virgin P ($11 per kilogram) and recycled P (50 cents per kilogram at an 80 percent recycling level) to be correct, then it would be expected that a higher level of recycling would result because at 50 cents per kilogram, recycled P costs are much lower than virgin costs. An increase in recycling under these conditions would further reduce the real per capita costs of phosphorus. As the level of recycling increased, the cost per kilogram would be increased. Eventually the cost per kilogram of recycled P would, at the margin, become approximately equal to the cost of virgin P.

It should be clear from this discussion as well as from the fact that the costs of P alone are being estimated that these cost estimates cannot be used to find the optimal amounts of land, recycling or synthesized food to feed any given population at minimum cost or even be used to choose one alternative over another.

Appendix A: Exhaustion Period Calculations and Supplementary Tables[1]

Calculation of the 2.7 Rule Estimates

A Simplified Example. In the first section of Chapter 1, the result of the original TIE report that phosphorus reserves would be depleted in sixty years was cited. This was based on a 1968 world phosphorus fertilizer consumption of 7.6 million metric tons,[2] deposits of 3.14 billion metric tons of P, and a world population growing at 1.9 percent per year. The simplest explanation of this calculation is as follows.

In the first year 7.6 million tons of P are used. In the second year population is 1.9 percent larger; by the 2.7 power rule, which states that fertilizer use must increase 2.7 times faster than the population if crop output is to keep pace with population growth, fertilizer use must be increased 2.7 times 1.9, or 5.13 percent. Therefore, 7.6 million times 1.0513 tons of P fertilizer are used. In the third year population is again 1.9 percent larger than the second year and fertilizer use must again be increased by 5.13 percent over the second year; third-year consumption of P fertilizer is then 7.6 million $(1.0513)^2$. Fourth-year use will be 7.6 million $(1.0513)^3$, and so on. The exhaustion date is that time when the sum of cumulative consumption of P equals 3,140 million tons of P, or $7.6 + 7.6 (1.0513) + 7.6 (1.0513)^2 + 7.6 (1.0513)^3 + \ldots 7.6 (1.0513)^n = 3,140$. The object is to determine n,

71

the exhaustion date. Since the terms on the left side form a geometric series, the expression reduces to

$$(7.6) \quad \left[\frac{(1.0513)^{n+1} - 1}{0.0513}\right] = 3{,}140, \text{ and } n \text{ is found to be 61.}$$

While this illustration treats each year's consumption in a discrete manner, the results in Chapter 1 and elsewhere in the text were really obtained from continuous forms based on exponential growth rates. This latter approach expedites the math and is more realistic, but the differences in results between the two methods is small.

Exponential Derivation. To illustrate the exponential version of these calculations, the consumption figure in the revised version edition—namely, a 1968 production of 11.3 million tons of P—is employed.

The basic 2.7 rule formula for annual production (mining) of phosphorus is: $N^{2.7} = kZ$, where N is population in billions and Z is annual production of P in millions of metric tons. The constant, k, is determined by noting that with $N = N_0 = 3.6$, Z is 11.3. Therefore,

$$k = \frac{3.6^{2.7}}{11.3} = 2.81 \,; \text{ or } N^{2.7} = 2.81Z. \tag{1}$$

If population increases at 1.9 percent per year, then population at any time $= N_0 e^{rt}$,

$$N = 3.6 e^{0.019t} \tag{2}$$

where time, t, is measured in years with $t = 0$ in 1968 when the world population was 3.6 billion. The cumulative use or production of phosphorus over any time interval 0 to T is given by:

$$Q = \int_0^T Z dt = \int_0^T \frac{N^{2.7}}{2.81} dt = \int_0^T \frac{(3.6 e^{0.019t})^{2.7}}{2.81} dt$$
$$= \int_0^T 11.3 e^{0.0513 t} dt = \left(\frac{11.3}{0.0513}\right)(e^{0.0513 t} - 1)$$
$$Q = 220.27 \,(e^{0.0513 T} - 1) \tag{3}$$

where Q is cumulative usage of P in millions of metric tons over time period T.

Suppose that the reserve of P is 20,000 million tons. How long would that reserve last if population continues to grow at 1.9 percent per year? Q is set to 20,000 in Equation 3, and is solved to determine the run-out date:

$$20,000 = 220.27 \ (e^{0.0513T} - 1).$$
$$e^{0.0513T} = 91.80, \text{ or } T = 88 \text{ years.}$$

In eighty-eight years the cumulative use of P is 20,000 million tons under the assumptions provided, and this agrees with the (rounded) TIE estimate of ninety years. From Equation 2, $N = 3.6e^{0.019\ t}$, the world population at the end of eighty-eight years would be about 19 billion. And from Equation 1, $N^{2.7} = 2.8Z$, the annual use of P at the exhaustion time of eighty-eight years with a population of 19 billion would be 1,040 million tons per year.

Most of the entries in columns 4 through 9 of Table 1 were obtained from these equations.[3] The example provided above is illustrative of a constant population growth case: the population grows at an annual 1.9 percent rate until it exhausts the designated recoverable reserve of P.

In contrast, it is possible to assume that the population rises to a certain level, say, 12 billion, and then instantly levels off. The same basic formulas are used to calculate exhaustion times but in a slightly different way. For example, for a 12 billion ultimate population and a 20,000 million ton reserve, the time to reach 12 billion population is calculated from Equation 2. This is sixty-three years. Then the cumulative usage of P during these sixty-three years is calculated by Equation 3. The answer (5,460 million tons) is subtracted from the total initial reserve of 20,000 million tons. This remaining reserve of 14,500 million tons is then consumed at the annual rate of about 290 million tons per year (calculated from Equation 1 for a population of 12 billion people) so it lasts an additional fifty years (14,500 million tons of remaining reserve divided by 290 million tons per year). The total exhaustion time is then 63 plus 50 years, or 110 years.

FAO Equation Calculations

Annual Usage Calculations. The basic FAO prediction equation is

$$V = 85.04 + 0.2496F + 12.51\sqrt{F} \qquad (4)$$

where V is the annual yield-value index per hectare and F is the annual fertilizer application in kilograms per hectare. Fertilizer is defined in terms of kilograms of nitrogen (N), phosphate (P_2O_5), and potash (K_2O).

As explained in the text, in 1970 the average worldwide value for F was approximately 45 kg. per hectare per year. Substitution of this value into Equation 4 yields a value of 180.2 for V. This value of V was "equated" to the 1968 world population of 3.6 billion people and was assumed to change proportionally. For example, a 10 percent increase in population is assumed to require a 10 percent increase in V. Since F is in terms of all fertilizer used per hectare, a simple constant proportion of this is assumed to be phosphorus. Quite simply, then, a value for F of 45 was treated as the equivalent of a worldwide production of phosphorus of 11.3 million tons, and increases in F were assumed to increase production of P proportionately. Thus

$$Z = (11.3/45)F = 0.2511F \qquad (5)$$

where Z is the annual world production of P in millions of metric tons.

Before annual total use of P can be calculated for any given size of population, Equation 4 must be solved in terms of F. Equation 4 is of quadratic form for the $\sqrt{F}$:

$$0.2496(\sqrt{F})^2 + 12.51\sqrt{F} + (85.04 - V) = 0 \qquad (6)$$

Using the standard formula, the $\sqrt{F}$ can be solved for:

$$\sqrt{F} = \frac{-12.51 \pm \sqrt{(12.51)^2 - (4)(0.2496)(85.04 - V)}}{2(0.2496)} \qquad (7)$$

Using the positive root and squaring:

$$F = [(12.51)^2 - (2)(12.51)\sqrt{(12.51)^2 - 4(0.2496)(85.04 - V)} + (12.51)^2 - 4(0.2496)(85.04 - V)] \div [(4)(0.2496)^2] \qquad (8)$$

For any given world population, N, in billions,

$$V = \left(\frac{N}{3.6}\right) 180.2 \qquad (9)$$

This value of V is used in Equation 8 to determine F, and thence by way of Equation 5 to determine Z, the annual total consumption (adjusted upward for production losses) of P.

For example, if the world population is 20 billion, then the corresponding value of V from Equation 9 is 1,001. Substitution of this value of V into Equation 8 indicates a projected annual fertilizer use of 1,640 kg. per arable hectare, or, by means of Equation 5, the annual total world production of P is estimated to be 412 million tons.

Cumulative FAO Usage Calculations. The cumulative use of P over any time period, T, measured from 1968 if the population starts at 3.6 billion in 1968 and grows at a constant 1.9 percent annual rate (as in Equation 2), is given by

$$Q = \int_0^T Z_t dt = (0.2511) \int_0^T F_t dt \tag{10}$$

where Q is millions of tons P produced over the period T, starting in 1968. Since N is given by $N = 3.6e^{0.019t}$, V also grows at the same rate so that from Equation 9:

$$V = (e^{0.019t})(180.2) \tag{11}$$

and this must be substituted into Equation 8. In order to simplify the presentation, the following substitutions have been made:

$$k = 0.2511 \qquad c = 85.04$$

$$a = 0.2496 \qquad d = 180.2$$

$$b = 12.51 \qquad g = 0.019$$

Substituting Equation 11 into Equation 8 gives:

$$F_t = [b^2 - 2b\sqrt{b^2 - 4a(c - de^{gt})} + b^2 - 4a(c - de^{gt})]/(4a^2)$$

or, rearranging terms,

$$F_t = \frac{(2b^2 - 4ac) - (2b\sqrt{(b^2 - 4ac) + 4ade^{gt}}) + (4ade^{gt})}{4a^2} \tag{12}$$

To simplify further, let

$$h = (2b^2 - 4ac) \qquad n = 4ad$$

$$j = (b^2 - 4ac) \qquad m = 4a^2$$

Then

$$F_t = [h - 2b\sqrt{j + ne^{gt}} + ne^{gt}]/m \tag{13}$$

Substituting into (10):

$$
\begin{aligned}
Q &= \frac{k}{m}\left[h\int_0^T dt - 2b\int_0^T (\sqrt{j + ne^{gt}})dt + n\int_0^T (e^{gt})dt\right] \\
&= \frac{k}{m}\left[hT - 2b\int_0^T (\sqrt{j + ne^{gt}})dt + \frac{n}{g}(e^{gt} - 1)\right]
\end{aligned}
\tag{14}
$$

To evaluate the middle integral, let $u = e^{gt}$, then $du = (ge^{gt})dt$ and $dt = \dfrac{du}{gu}$. Also, when $t = 0$, $u = 1$, and when $t = T$, $u = e^{gT}$. Thus:

$$\int_0^T (\sqrt{j + ne^{gt}})dt = \frac{1}{g}\int_1^{e^{gt}} \left(\frac{\sqrt{j + nu}}{u}\right)du$$

(reducible by standard formulas to)

$$
= \left(\frac{1}{g}\right)\left\{2(\sqrt{j + nu}) + j\left[\left(\frac{1}{\sqrt{j}}\right)\log\left(\frac{\sqrt{j + nu} - \sqrt{j}}{\sqrt{j + nu} + \sqrt{j}}\right)\right]\right\}_1^{e^{gt}}
$$

$$
\begin{aligned}
= \left(\frac{1}{g}\right)&\left\{2\left[\sqrt{j + ne^{gT}} - \sqrt{j + n}\right]\right. \\
&\left. + \sqrt{j}\left[\log\left(\frac{\sqrt{j + ne^{gT}} - \sqrt{j}}{\sqrt{j + ne^{gT}} + \sqrt{j}}\right) - \log\left(\frac{\sqrt{j + n} - \sqrt{j}}{\sqrt{j + n} + \sqrt{j}}\right)\right]\right\}
\end{aligned}
\tag{15}
$$

where log indicates natural logs. If we let $o = \sqrt{j + n}$, and $v = \sqrt{j + ne^{gT}}$, then substitution of Equation 15 into Equation 14 yields:

$$
\begin{aligned}
Q = \frac{k}{m}&\left\{hT + \frac{n}{g}(e^{gT} - 1) - \left(\frac{2b}{g}\right)\left[2(v - o)\right.\right. \\
&\left.\left. + \sqrt{j}\left(\log\left\{\frac{v - \sqrt{j}}{v + \sqrt{j}}\right\} - \log\left\{\frac{o - \sqrt{j}}{o + \sqrt{j}}\right\}\right)\right]\right\}
\end{aligned}
\tag{16}
$$

Substituting back all the numeric constants and simplifying:

$$
\begin{aligned}
Q = 19{,}180 + 1.008 &\left\{228.1T + 9469e^{gT}\right. \\
&- 1316.8\left[2\sqrt{71.60 + 179.9e^{gT}}\right. \\
&\left.\left. + 8.461\log\left(\frac{\sqrt{71.60 + 179.9e^{gT}} - 8.461}{\sqrt{71.60 + 179.9e^{gT}} + 8.461}\right)\right]\right\}
\end{aligned}
\tag{17}
$$

All that is necessary to determine Q, the cumulative production of P in millions of tons over any designated period of time, starting at 1968 with a world population of 3.6 billion and growing at a rate of 1.9 percent per year, is to designate the interval period T in years.[4] For example, for the cumulative usage between 1968 and the time (at an annual growth rate of 1.9 percent) when the population reaches 12 billion, T is determined to be 63.4 years from Equation 2, and this value is inserted into Equation 17. The cumulative use of P over the 63.4 years is found to be 4,400 million tons.

FAO Exhaustion Period Calculations. The remaining calculations for Table 2 follow from this point those for Table 1. For example, for an ultimate population of 12 billion people, we have already determined that the cumulative use of P during the sixty-three years the population grows from 3.6 billion to 12 billion is, from Equation 17, 4,400 million tons. By means of equations 9, 8, and 5, the annual amount of P mined for a population of 12 billion is about 180 million tons or about 15 kg. of P per capita per year. If the initial reserve of P were 20,000 million tons in 1968, the remainder after sixty-three years when the population became 12 billion would be 15,600 million tons (20,000 − 4,400) which would last another eighty-six years at the rate of 180 million tons per year. According to the modified FAO formula, the total time to exhaust the 20 billion tons of P would then be about 150 years for an ultimate population size of 12 billion.

Additional Tables for Chapter 5

Table 4 in Chapter 5 provides rough estimates on exhaustion periods and annual mined phosphorus costs per capita for several reserve estimates and several alternative usage projection formulas or rules for a stable world population of 20 billion. The population growth period is ignored in these calculations for the sake of simplicity. Tables A-1, A-2, and A-3 are based on the same format as Table 4 except for stable world populations of 12, 50, and 100 billion people, respectively.

TABLE A–1. Exhaustion Times and Per Capita Costs Under Various Alternative Phosphorus Fertilizer Consumption Assumptions (for a Constant-Size World Population of 12 Billion)

Projection formula[a]	Net annual use (million tons) (1)	Net annual per capita use (kg.) (Col. 1 ÷ 12 bill.) (2)	Exhaustion periods recoverable	
			20 billion tons (3)	180 billion tons (4)
2.7 rule				
1. Base case	292.0	24.3	69	617
2. 80% recycle	58.0	4.9	343	3,090
3. 2X land	90.0	7.5	223	2,010
4. 80% recycle, 2X land	18.0	1.5	1,110	10,000
FAO formula				
5. Base case	181.0	15.1	111	995
6. 80% recycle	36.0	3.0	553	4,970
7. 2X land	92.0	7.7	217	1,950
8. 80% recycle, 2X land	18.0	1.5	1,080	9,760
20 kg. per capita				
9. Base case	240.0	20.0	83	750
10. 80% recycle	48.0	4.0	417	3,750
10 kg. per capita				
11. Base case	120.0	10.0	167	1,500
12. 80% recycle	24.0	2.0	833	7,500
0.7 kg. per capita				
13. Base case	8.4	0.7	2,380	21,400
14. 80% recycle	1.7	0.14	11,900	107,000

[a] 2X land indicates a doubling of arable land.

[b] Exhaustion periods are calculated by dividing the indicated deposit quantity by the corresponding net annual use in Column 1. (For Column 3: 20×10^9 ÷ Column 1; for Column 4: 180×10^9 ÷ Column 1; for Column 5: 30×10^{12} ÷ Column 1; for Column 6: 590×10^{12} ÷ Column 1.)

Because predicted annual consumption is lower for all those years in which the population is less than the ultimate level (20 billion in Table 4), the exhaustion times are longer than shown in Table 4 and Tables A-1, A-2, and A-3, where the population growth period has been ignored. As can be seen in tables 1 and 2, exhaustion periods are considerably extended in percentage terms for the 20- and 180-billion ton cases (columns 3 and 4) but are insignificantly greater for the 30- and 590-trillion ton cases (columns 5 and 6). For example, from Table 4 in

(years) for indicated deposits of P[b]		Annual per capita cost[c]			
30 trillion tons (5)	590 trillion tons (6)	Assumed cost ($/ton) (7)	Annual per capita cost (Col. 2 × Col. 7 ÷ 10³) (8)	Assumed cost ($/ton) (9)	Annual per capita cost (Col. 2 × Col. 9 ÷ 10³) (10)
103,000	2,020,000	$ 50	$1.22	$11,000	$267.00
514,000	10,100,000	2,000	9.72	13,000	63.20
334,000	6,570,000	50	0.37	11,000	82.30
1,670,000	32,900,000	2,000	2.98	13,000	19.40
166,000	3,260,000	50	0.75	11,000	166.00
829,000	16,300,000	2,000	6.03	13,000	39.20
325,000	6,400,000	50	0.38	11,000	84.50
1,630,000	32,000,000	2,000	3.07	13,000	20.00
125,000	2,460,000	50	1.00	11,000	220.00
625,000	12,300,000	2,000	8.00	13,000	52.00
250,000	4,920,000	50	0.50	11,000	110.00
1,250,000	24,600,000	2,000	4.00	13,000	26.00
3,570,000	70,200,000	50	0.04	11,000	7.70
17,900,000	351,000,000	2,000	0.28	13,000	1.82

[c] Costs in columns 7 and 8 should be associated with the deposit quantities indicated in columns 3–5; costs in columns 9 and 10 should be associated with deposit quantities in Column 6. All costs are partial; see text.

Chapter 5, the exhaustion period for a stable population of 20 billion and deposits of 20 billion tons is 17 years under the 2.7 rule (Table 4, line 1, column 3) and 49 years under the FAO equation (line 5, column 3). In contrast for calculations with growing populations, the 20 billion tons is exhausted in 88 years under the 2.7 rule (Table 1, line 4, column 5—but note that 20 billion tons is exhausted before the population reaches 20 billion), and in 110 years under the FAO equation (Table 2, line 4, column 5). However, for the 30-trillion ton deposit

TABLE A–2. Exhaustion Times and Per Capita Costs Under Various Alternative Phosphorus Fertilizer Consumption Assumptions (for a Constant-Size World Population of 50 Billion)

| | | | Exhaustion periods recoverable | |
| | Net annual use (million tons) (1) | Net annual per capita use (kg.) (Col. 1 ÷ 50 bill.) (2) | 20 billion tons (3) | 180 billion tons (4) |
Projection formula[a]				
2.7 rule				
1. Base case	13,700	275.0	1.5	13
2. 80% recycle	2,750	55.0	7.0	65
3. 2X land	4,230	84.6	5.0	43
4. 80% recycle, 2X land	846	16.9	24.0	213
FAO formula				
5. Base case	1,470	29.4	14.0	122
6. 80% recycle	294	5.9	68.0	612
7. 2X land	1,140	22.9	17.0	157
8. 80% recycle, 2X land	229	4.6	87.0	786
20 kg. per capita				
9. Base case	1,000	20.0	20.0	180
10. 80% recycle	200	4.0	100.0	900
10 kg. per capita				
11. Base case	500	10.0	40.0	360
12. 80% recycle	100	2.0	200.0	1,800
0.7 kg. per capita				
13. Base case	35	0.7	571.0	5,140
14. 80% recycle	7	0.14	2,860.0	25,700

  [a] 2X land indicates a doubling of arable land.
  [b] Exhaustion periods are calculated by dividing the indicated deposit quantity by the corresponding net annual use in Column 1. (For Column 3: 20×10^9 ÷ Column 1; for Column 4: 180×10^9 ÷ Column 1; for Column 5: 30×10^{12} ÷ Column 1; for Column 6: 590×10^{12} ÷ Column 1.)

calculations, the 2.7 rule yields an exhaustion period of 26,000 years in Table 1 (line 10, column 5) and 25,900 years in Table 4 (line 1, column 5); the FAO equation results are 72,900 years in Table 2 (line 10, column 5) and 72,800 years in Table 4 (line 5, column 5).

Calculation Methods.   Most of the calculations have already been explained above. In addition, since the population growth period is ignored, the calculations are much simplified. For the basic 2.7 rule

(years) for indicated deposits of P^b		Annual per capita cost[c]			
30 trillion tons (5)	590 trillion tons (6)	Assumed cost ($/ton) (7)	Annual per capita cost (Col. 2 × Col. 7 ÷ 10^3) (8)	Assumed cost ($/ton) (9)	Annual per capita cost (Col. 2 × Col. 9 ÷ 10^3) (10)
2,180	42,900	$ 50	$ 13.70	$11,000	$3,020.00
10,900	215,000	2,000	110.00	13,000	715.00
7,090	139,000	50	4.23	11,000	931.00
35,400	697,000	2,000	33.90	13,000	220.00
20,400	402,000	50	1.47	11,000	323.00
102,000	2,010,000	2,000	11.80	13,000	76.40
26,200	515,000	50	1.14	11,000	252.00
131,000	2,580,000	2,000	9.16	13,000	59.50
30,000	590,000	50	1.00	11,000	220.00
150,000	2,950,000	2,000	8.00	13,000	52.00
60,000	1,180,000	50	0.50	11,000	110.00
300,000	5,900,000	2,000	4.00	13,000	26.00
857,000	16,900,000	50	0.04	11,000	7.70
4,290,000	84,300,000	2,000	0.28	13,000	1.82

[c] Costs in columns 7 and 8 should be associated with the deposit quantities indicated in columns 3–5; costs in columns 9 and 10 should be associated with deposit quantities in Column 6. All costs are partial; see text.

calculation (line 1) for a given population, Equation 1 can be used to estimate annual world usage, and the exhaustion time calculation is then, as indicated in the tables themselves, a simple division. Annual per capita use and cost are also simple divisions and multiplications as indicated directly in the table. For the basic FAO rule (line 5), equations 9 (to find V for a given N), 8 (to find F for the corresponding V), and 5 (to find Z, the annual use of P, from F) are employed, and the rest follows as above. For the 20 kg., 10 kg., and 0.7 kg. rules, it is

TABLE A–3. Exhaustion Times and Per Capita Costs Under Various Alternative Phosphorus Fertilizer Consumption Assumptions (for a Constant-Size World Population of 100 Billion)

Projection formula[a]	Net annual use (million tons) (1)	Net annual per capita use (kg.) (Col. 1 ÷ 100 bill.) (2)	Exhaustion periods recoverable	
			20 billion tons (3)	180 billion tons (4)
2.7 rule				
1. Base case	89,300	893.0	0.2	2
2. 80% recycle	17,900	179.0	1.0	10
3. 2X land	27,500	275.0	0.7	7
4. 80% recycle, 2X land	5,500	55.0	4.0	32
FAO formula				
5. Base case	3,470	34.7	6.0	52
6. 80% recycle	694	6.9	29.0	259
7. 2X land	2,940	29.4	7.0	61
8. 80% recycle, 2X land	588	5.9	34.0	306
20 kg. per capita				
9. Base case	2,000	20.0	10.0	90
10. 80% recycle	400	4.0	50.0	450
10 kg. per capita				
11. Base case	1,000	10.0	20.0	180
12. 80% recycle	200	2.0	100.0	900
0.7 kg. per capita				
13. Base case	70	0.7	286.0	2,570
14. 80% recycle	14	0.14	1,430.0	12,900

[a] 2X land indicates a doubling of arable land.

[b] Exhaustion periods are calculated by dividing the indicated deposit quantity by the corresponding net annual use in Column 1. (For Column 3: 20×10^9 ÷ Column 1; for Column 4: 180×10^9 ÷ Column 1; for Column 5: 30×10^{12} ÷ Column 1; for Column 6: 590×10^{12} ÷ Column 1.)

merely necessary to multiply by the given population size to obtain annual worldwide usage estimates before proceeding to make the exhaustion period and per capita cost calculations.

Calculations for doubling of the arable land involve finding the annual use for half the given population from the FAO or 2.7 rule and then doubling that figure to account for both halves of the population. That is, for the 20 billion population case, doubling the arable land is equivalent to setting up two worlds, each with 10 billion people

(years) for indicated deposits of P^b		Annual per capita cost^c			
			Annual per capita cost (Col. 2 × Col. 7 ÷ 10³)		Annual per capita cost (Col. 2 × Col. 9 ÷ 10³)
30 trillion tons (5)	590 trillion tons (6)	Assumed cost ($/ton) (7)	(8)	Assumed cost ($/ton) (9)	(10)
336	6,600	$ 50	$ 44.70	$11,000	$9,830.00
1,680	33,000	2,000	357.00	13,000	2,320.00
1,090	21,500	50	13.70	11,000	3,020.00
5,450	107,000	2,000	110.00	13,000	715.00
8,640	170,000	50	1.74	11,000	382.00
43,200	850,000	2,000	13.90	13,000	90.20
10,200	201,000	50	1.47	11,000	323.00
51,000	1,000,000	2,000	11.80	13,000	76.40
15,000	295,000	50	1.00	11,000	220.00
75,000	1,480,000	2,000	8.00	13,000	52.00
30,000	590,000	50	0.50	11,000	110.00
150,000	2,950,000	2,000	4.00	13,000	26.00
429,000	8,430,000	50	0.04	11,000	7.70
2,140,000	42,100,000	2,000	0.28	13,000	1.82

^{c} Costs in columns 7 and 8 should be associated with the deposit quantities indicated in columns 3–5; costs in columns 9 and 10 should be associated with deposit quantities in Column 6. All costs are partial; see text.

but with the original amount of arable land (1,400 million ha.) on each. By their nature the 20, 10, and 0.7 kg. rules are not affected by doubling the amount of land (although doubling the arable land would certainly affect the total population supportable on earth—in accordance with De Wit's calculations, it is assumed that this is at least 20 billion people).

The 80 percent recycle net annual usage estimates were derived by dividing the corresponding non-recycle estimates by 5. For example, the 2.7 rule indicates an annual use of 1,160 million metric tons for a population of 20 billion (Table 4, line 1, column 1). The gross use with 80 percent recycling is still 1,160 million tons, but only 20 percent of this is newly mined each year so the net utilization of the recoverable deposits is 20 percent of 1,160, or 230 million tons per year (Table 4, line 2, column 1).

Definition of 80 Percent Recycling. The "80 percent recycling" phrase requires some explanation. Some level of recycling is already practiced through the use of manure fertilizing, and the 2.7 rule and the FAO formula implicitly take this into account. Thus, for these two projection formulas, 80 percent recycling means recycling 80 percent of whatever is not now being recycled.

Suppose gross annual consumption of phosphorus fertilizer in all forms is 10 million tons and 2 million tons is recycled, mainly from animal manures. Then 80 percent recycling would mean recycling 80 percent of the remaining 8 million tons, or 6.4 tons. Total annual recycling would then be 8.4 tons, or a total recycling percentage of 84 percent.

The concept is really even less defined than this example implies since it is unclear what happens as gross use increases. If gross annual consumption increases from 10 million tons to 20 million tons, some assumption must be made about the "usual" recycling percentage or amount. At one extreme, it could be assumed the "ordinary" manure recycling remains at 2 million tons per year, so an additional 80 percent recycling would be 80 percent of 18 million tons, or 14.4 tons per year. At the other extreme, it could be assumed manure recycling increases in proportion to 4 million tons per year, so that an additional 80 percent recycling implies an increase of 80 percent of 16 million tons, or 12.8 tons per year.

To understand what is actually implied it is necessary to examine the data underlying the FAO and 2.7 prediction rules. In both cases, the higher use of fertilizer is associated with the more-developed countries where the percentage of recycling is less. If these formulas had been based on organic as well as inorganic plant nutrient sources, then the measured nutrient applications in less-developed countries would have been increased relatively more and even less response in output to increased fertilizer applications would have resulted. Aside from this deficiency in these two projection formulas, the association of more inorganic fertilizer with less organic recycling implies a falling off in the "usual" or "background" level of recycling. Therefore, the background level imputed by either formula to populations of 12 billion or more is probably quite small.

This ambiguity does not exist for the 20, 10, or 0.7 kg. rules as these predictors are based on total "requirements," independent of source. Whether the source is organic or inorganic phosphorus has little effect on the result (although manures help in reducing soil erosion and runoff).

The selection of the 80 percent figure for a recycling level obviously involves a certain amount of arbitrariness. The level of recycling is clearly a function of cost. At a higher cost, a higher percentage will be recycled. From the section on recycling in Chapter 4 and the cost per ton assumed, it seems that 80 percent recycling is perhaps reasonable.

Costs Per Ton.   Costs per metric ton of phosphorus again represent the costs of mining and (onsite) beneficiating the ore to the level necessary for processing into phosphate fertilizer. They do not include transport costs to the fertilizer plant. The $50 and $11,000 costs for the nonrecycled cases have already been discussed in connection with Tables 1 and 2.

The average cost of each metric ton of recycled phosphorus was assumed to be $500. Since much phosphorus can be recycled at significantly lower costs (e.g., manure, other organics, direct use of sewage), this average figure includes a high percentage of low-cost recycled phosphorus and a small percentage of very expensive recycled phosphorus (e.g., erosion control). Of course, the average cost will be a function of the percentage recycled. To recycle 100 percent of all phosphorus in manure would, of course, become very expensive. At the same time, the cost to prevent the loss of, say, a total of only 0.1 percent of the phosphorus potentially lost from soil erosion might be much less than recycling 99.9 percent of phosphorus in manure on a per-ton cost basis. Nevertheless, from the figures derived in the soil erosion control and the recycling sections, it would appear that an average of $500 per ton would be compatible with an (additional) 80 percent recycling level.

The cost per ton of *net* annual use for an 80 percent recycling level is derived by averaging the cost of 4 tons of recycled phosphorus with 1 ton of virgin phosphorus. For the 20-billion, 180-billion, and 30-trillion ton examples, the virgin cost is assumed to be $50 per metric ton. For every ton of virgin phosphorus, 4 tons of recycled are needed at $500 per ton. The average price of the mix would be about $2,000 per ton. It is perhaps easier to follow this on a gross use basis. Each net ton of use is equivalent, as explained, to 5 gross tons. The cost of 5 gross tons is $2,050—4 recycled tons at $500 and 1 virgin ton at $50. Thus, each net ton of use costs $2,050 (or rounded, $2,000). For the 590-trillion ton common rock reserve, the 4 gross tons cost $2,000 and the 1 virgin ton $11,000, for a total of $13,000 per net ton.

It should be cautioned again that these are not the complete costs of adopting each alternative. For example, costs of land preparation or irrigation are not shown for doubling the arable land area. Similarly, the costs of synthesized food might be larger or smaller than existing conventional food costs at some time in the future but this is not estimated here either (for the 0.7 kg. per capita cases on lines 13 and 14). The focus is on the critical element of concern—phosphorus. It is assumed, then, that the other costs not shown will be bearable if the per capita cost of phosphorus can be borne. But for this reason the selection of one alternative over another cannot be made on the basis of the phosphorus costs (even if they were accurately predicted).

Notes

[1] In many cases the numeric answers provided here will diverge slightly from the answers one might obtain by performing the indicated calculations. This is because the numbers have been rounded off. The actual calculations were performed by computer so additional, spurious, decimal places were calculated. Although several places are provided within the text, no answer has more than one or two significant digits.

[2] Later figures are available but the 1968 year base is employed in order to maintain consistency with the TIE study.

³ This does not include the first two rows, which were based on the 1968 P usage of 7.6 million tons as in the original 1971 TIE report rather than the revised TIE figure of 11.3 million tons per year. The same equations apply for the top two lines except for this change in constant.

⁴ A numerical year-by-year cumulation was performed by computer to check the accuracy of Equation 17 (as well as to check the accuracy of the actual program used in place of Equation 17), and the answers provided by both methods were in agreement. This indicates that in the mechanical, mathematical sense Equation 17 is correct.

Appendix B:
The 2.7 Power Equation
for Estimating
Fertilizer Use Levels

Derivation of the 2.7 Rule

The 2.7 power rule states that fertilizer use must increase 2.7 times as fast as agricultural output. The TIE group attributes the origin of this prediction rule to a study by the President's Science Advisory Committee (PSAC).[1] In estimating the future use of pesticides for the PSAC study, the group concerned with this problem (W. B. Ennis, Jr., L. L. Jansen, I. T. Ellis, and L. D. Newsom) also incidentally provided a regression estimate of crop yields versus fertilizers.[2] They plotted on log-log paper the average yields per hectare of principal food crops against average fertilizer usage in aggregate kilograms of nitrogen (N), phosphate (P_2O_5), and potash (K_2O) per hectare for three dates (1952, 1957–58, and 1962–63) in three countries (India, Japan, and the United States). From these nine data points they found, with a coefficient of determination (R^2) of 0.98, that $\log F = 2.716 \log Y - 7.612$, where F is average annual fertilizer usage in kilograms per hectare and Y is the average annual food crop yield in kilograms per hectare (and the logs are in the base 10). This equation can be converted into exponential form by noting that 7.612 equals the log of 4.1×10^7. Thus, $F = Y^{2.716}/(4.1 \times 10^7)$, which yields the 2.7 rule.

Causal Relationships. One major problem of this analysis is the implicit assumption that fertilizer alone is responsible for crop output levels. Ennis et al. provide immediate evidence to the contrary by correlating the log of per hectare yields against the log of per hectare pesticide use for the same nine observations. The coefficient of determination in this regression is 0.95—indicating that pesticides alone are responsible for crop output levels. It is clearly wrong to make either assumption.[3] Crop output per hectare is a function of fertilizer, pesticides, irrigation, seed varieties, man-hours of labor, machine inputs, level of efficiency, soils, climate, and other variables.[4] Thus, merely increasing fertilizer alone (or pesticide alone) without increasing any other input would probably lead to much smaller increases than the 2.7 rule implies. On the other hand, increases in output might be achieved to some extent without any increase in fertilizer, if other inputs were increased.

The high correlation coefficients for fertilizer and pesticide alone merely indicate that increased output is usually associated with increases in both. Increased use of fertilizer (or pesticide) is also a good indication that there have been increases in other inputs as well, since it is commonly noted that a high level of fertilizer use is usually an indicator of overall advanced agricultural management practices. Thus, while fertilizer input may be used as a measure of all inputs in the 2.7 rule, it does not tell us what we are interested in—namely, what happens as the relative price of P fertilizer goes up in high output situations. Although it is true that to achieve higher agricultural output all inputs must be increased, it may be that at high output levels *and* higher phosphate fertilizer prices, the latter will be conserved to a much greater degree than under current practices. We really want to know more about the possible range of phosphate fertilizer input for high levels of crop production rather than the current average input of phosphate fertilizer for high levels of output.

For the purposes at hand, it would be better (if the input collinearity problem could be overcome) to have a multiple correlation study in order to see what levels of output could be achieved without increasing the level of phosphate fertilization very much, but with increases in other inputs. Such a comprehensive analysis has not come to our attention. However, the usefulness of a multiple regression would probably still be limited because conditions of high output with high phosphate costs would not be part of the data used for such a regression.

Additional Regressions on the PSAC Data. In order to examine this problem in more detail, regressions of per hectare output as a function of both fertilizer and pesticide were made.[5] Because the nine data points were not tabulated in the PSAC study, it was first necessary to read the data off three graphs. To check whether these graphical data were accurate, the regression of the $\log_{10}$ of output per hectare ($\log Y$) as a function of the $\log_{10}$ of fertilizer per hectare ($\log F$) was estimated. The results were close enough to those obtained by Ennis et al. to validate the data for further analysis. Instead of the $\log F = 2.716$ $\log Y - 7.612$ (with $R^2 = 0.98$) reported by Ennis et al., the regression relationship from the nine sets of observations read off graphs was $\log F = 2.707 \log Y - 7.578$.

$$(17.24) \qquad\qquad (14.63) \qquad\qquad\qquad\qquad\qquad (R^2 = 0.97).[6]$$

Because the data from the graphs appeared to be acceptably close to the original data,[7] the regression of the log of Y as a function of the log of F and the log of D (grams of pesticide per hectare) was run. The resulting equation is: $\log Y = 2.811 - 0.000383 \log D + 0.3613 \log F$.

$$(10.58) \quad (0.002) \qquad\qquad (2.189)$$
$$(R^2 = 0.97).$$

The last regression leads to the conclusion that pesticides are not an important explanatory variable in predicting output; worse, pesticides evidently reduce output and the confidence that pesticide and fertilizer help increase crop output is much smaller (i.e., the t ratios are much smaller).[8] Such nonsense results tend to vitiate the basis for the 2.7 rule. The correlation between pesticides and fertilizer use is so high (with $R^2 = 0.98$ according to Ennis et al.) that it is really not possible to sort these two inputs from each other as they are evidently used in conjunction with each other (as well as with other modern management practices). Therefore, the paucity of data and the high degree of correlation between fertilizers, pesticides and other inputs tend to undermine the 2.7 rule on a statistical basis.

Additional Weaknesses in the Derivation. Ennis et al. do discuss the point that such countrywide averages may disguise important details. For example, if one type of crop (in the "modern sector") receives most of the fertilizer, presumably the average crop yield can be increased by using the same amount of fertilizer (so the average fertilizer use remains the same) but using less on the one specialty crop and more on the less-fertilized crops. However, this discussion and all subsequent adjustments in the source study are carried out with respect to pesticides, not fertilizers.

The conclusion of Ennis et al. that the fertilizer-to-yield relationship is not greatly affected by other influences such as soil type and climate is striking but is also undermined by the lack of data. Although nine data points were used, the relatively close grouping of points for each country effectively reduces the number of data points to more like three. The three-yield figures for India range from 650 to 820 kg. per hectare, the three for the U.S., from 1,800 to 2,700 kg., and the three for Japan, from 4,000 to 5,500 kg. It is, of course, much easier to obtain a good fit with just three points. The way out of this particular shortcoming is to incorporate data on additional countries as has been done in the FAO study.

Recent Trends in the Data and the 2.7 Rule

Population-Based Predictions. It is claimed in the TIE report that the recent world population growth of 1.9 percent per year accompanied by a 5.25 percent per year increase in phosphate fertilizer use conforms well with the 2.7 power rule, since this rule would lead to a prediction that if the population increased 1.9 percent, phosphate fertilizer use would increase 5.2 percent.[9]

The calculations in Table B-1 indicate that over the 1954–55 to 1969–70 period, the 2.7 rule slightly underestimates the actual annual growth rate of phosphate fertilizer use but the agreement is rather good. However, the 2.7 rule is based on total fertilizer use including N, P_2O_5, and K_2O, and not just P_2O_5. In terms of all fertilizer, the 2.7 rule is not very good. The main problem seems to be that the price of nitrogen fertilizer has dropped significantly and its use correspondingly increased greatly.[10] The closeness between the predicted and the actual annual increase in phosphate fertilizer is evidently fortuitous since the only relevant test relates to all fertilizers. This also suggests that not

TABLE B-1. Actual and Predicted Fertilizer Use Growth Rates

	1954–55—1959–60 (%)	1959–60—1964–65 (%)	1964–65—1969–70 (%)	1954–55—1969–70 (%)
	Actual			
All fertilizer use[a]	5.87	7.53	7.80	7.07
Phosphate fertilizer use[a]	5.20	6.11	5.62	5.64
	Predicted by the 2.7 rule[b]			
World population[c]	(1.89) 5.11	(1.96) 5.29	(1.98) 5.36	(1.94) 5.25
Total agricultural output per hectare[c]	(2.49) 6.73	(1.79) 4.83	(2.64) 7.12	(2.29) 6.19
Adjustment for increase in arable land[c]	(0.56) 7.29	(0.27) 5.10	(0.06) 7.18	(0.30) 6.48

Sources: Various issues of the FAO's *Annual Fertilizer Review* and *Production Yearbook;* population figures from 1971 U.N. *Demographic Yearbook.*

[a] Includes rock phosphate applied directly, but excludes fertilizer use in China, North Vietnam, and North Korea because data for these countries were available from 1965–66 only.

[b] Figures in parentheses are annual rates of growth, in percentages, for the item in question—e.g., world population grew at an exponential rate of 1.89 percent per year for the period indicated. For "World population" and "Total agricultural output per hectare," the numbers not in parentheses are equal to 2.7 times the number in parentheses to the left—e.g., $1.89 \times 2.7 = 5.11$ percent. (Because of rounding the answer may differ slightly from the number indicated). For "Adjustment for increase in arable land," the numbers not in parentheses are obtained by adding the number in parentheses to the left to the predicted fertilizer growth rate from "Total agricultural output per hectare"—e.g., $6.73 + 0.56 = 7.29$ percent per year.

[c] Time periods for these items are 1955–60, 1960–65, 1965–70, and 1955–70.

only is the 2.7 rule not very accurate for predicting total fertilizer nutrient applications but it also requires additional assumptions (or additional analysis) concerning phosphate fertilizer.

Agricultural Output Per Capita[11].   Since the 2.7 rule actually applies to yields per arable hectare rather than world population, the translation to population involves the assumptions that the average diet remains the same and that the arable land remains constant. If the average diet has been improving, then basing the 2.7 rule on population rather than yields would lead to underestimates of fertilizer use.[12] FAO data indicate that per capita total food production for the world has increased about 12 percent over the 1955–70 period (0.8 percent per year) and 5 percent over the 1965–70 period (0.9 percent per year).[13] The same source indicates that per capita total agricultural farm production including food and nonfood crops (cotton, tobacco, etc.) has risen only 9 percent from 1955 to 1970 (0.6 percent per year) and 3 percent from 1965 to 1970 (0.6 percent per year).[14] The more relevant of these two measures is the total per capita agricultural production since fertilizer is applied to nonfood crops as well. Thus, the growth of world population understates the growth of per hectare yields (if arable land was constant over the period) by about 0.6 percent per year.

Changes in Arable Land.   Correspondingly, if the cultivated land increases, the output per hectare can decline to maintain the same level of production but the prediction of fertilizer use based on population would not reflect this. For the fifteen-year period from 1955 to 1970, the arable land reported by FAO has increased about 4.5 percent (0.3 percent per year) ; about 0.3 percent over the 1965–70 period (0.06 percent per year).[15] The data for arable land are not very reliable since the definition varies from country to country and year to year. Changes in arable land are often the result of improvements in land surveys rather than actual changes in the amount of arable land.[16] To the extent arable land did increase, the growth of world population overstates the growth of per hectare yields.

Output Per Arable Hectare Fertilizer Predictions.   The net influence
of increases in per capita total agricultural production and increases in
arable land is shown on line 4 of Table B-1. Here an index of total
agricultural output per hectare was obtained by dividing the FAO
total agricultural production index by the amount of arable land. Annual rates of increase in this index were then calculated for the periods
shown. The 2.7 rule was then applied to obtain the predicted annual
increase in per hectare fertilizer used.[17] Since the amount of arable land
was increasing, the predicted annual increases in the total world fertilizer applications would be the predicted increase in fertilizer per
hectare times the increase in arable land. These predictions, shown in
the last row, should be compared with the actual annual rates of increase in the first two rows.[18] These predictions are somewhat better
in terms of total fertilizer consumption but perhaps not as good for
total phosphate fertilizer consumption. The differences between projected and actual are perhaps acceptable for short-run phosphate
projections,[19] but over long periods of time might lead to *very* large
errors.

Notes

[1] President's Science Advisory Committee, Panel on the World Food Supply,
The World Food Problem (Washington, D.C.: Government Printing Office, 1967).

[2] Ibid., vol. 3, pp. 139–145.

[3] In defense of Ennis et al. it should be noted that they were simply interested in
determining the amount of pesticide and fertilizer associated with certain levels of
output and never imputed any causality. Problems only arise when projecting
inputs on this basis for quite different conditions.

[4] This point is discussed at length in Charles E. Kellogg and Arnold C. Orvedal,
"Potentially Arable Soils of the World and Critical Measures for their Use,"
Advances in Agronomy, vol. 21 (1969), pp. 112–122. They refer to the interrelation-
ship of inputs to achieve higher output (e.g., increased fertilization alone may bring
no additional crop output, and to obtain higher output may require additional
water, pesticide controls, weeding, etc., as well as more fertilizer) as the "Principle
of Interactions."

[5] These regressions were run by Toby Page of Resources for the Future, Inc. I
am also indebted to him for interpreting the results.

[6] The numbers in parentheses are the t ratios. The chances that either of these
coefficients is really zero are less than one-tenth of 1 percent.

Also notice that making output (Y) the independent variable and fertilizer (F)
the dependent variable expresses output as a function of fertilizer rather than vice
versa. If this is done, the coefficients are slightly different: $\log Y = 2.8108 +$

0.36093 log F, or when rearranged: $\log F = 2.771 \log Y - 7.788$. Thus, the 2.7 rule becomes a 2.77 rule, or, when rounded, a 2.8 rule.

[7] In addition to the check on the data from the regression of fertilizer as a function of output, the data extracted from the graphs were also checked with the results of the other two regressions provided in the PSAC pesticide study. For yield as a function of pesticides, $\log D = 2.575 \log Y - 5.683$ (with $R^2 = 0.95$) from the PSAC study, versus $\log D = 2.580 \log Y - 5.690$ (with $R^2 = 0.95$) from the data taken off graphs in the PSAC study. For pesticides as a function of fertilizer, $\log D = 0.949 \log F + 1.532$ (with $R^2 = 0.98$) from the PSAC study; versus $\log D = 0.953 \log F + 1.535$ (with $R^2 = 0.98$) from the graph data.

[8] The chance that the true coefficient of the log of pesticides is zero is over 90 percent. The chance that the true coefficient of the log of fertilizer is zero is between 5 and 10 percent.

[9] If $Z = kN^{2.7}$, where Z is the annual rate of P fertilizer consumption and N is the world population, then initially, $Z_0 = k(N_0)^{2.7}$. If population increases 1.9 percent, then $N_1 = 1.019 N_0$ and $Z_1 = k (1.019 N_0)^{2.7} = Z_0 (1.019)^{2.7} = 1.052 Z_0$, or Z_1 is 5.2 percent greater than Z_0.

[10] FAO, *Fertilizers: An Annual Review of World Production, Consumption, Trade and Prices—1969* (Rome: FAO, 1970), pp. 1 and 144; FAO *Annual Fertilizer Review: 1970* (Rome: FAO, 1971), pp. 6–7.

[11] *Agricultural output*, the term used by the FAO, means farm output and does not include the production of fertilizer, farm machinery, etc.

[12] To understand this, assume for simplicity that population (and land) does not increase but diet and, therefore, yields per hectare do. With fertilizer based on population, no increase in fertilizer would be indicated since there is no change in population. Based on yields per hectare, an increase in fertilizer is predicted.

[13] FAO, *Production Yearbook: 1970*, vol. 24 (Rome: FAO, 1971), Table 8; and *Production Yearbook: 1971*, vol. 25 (1972), Table 8. The index of per capita food production in 1955 was 101, and 112 in 1969 on a base of 100 for 1952–56; it was 104 for 1969 and 105 for 1970 on a base of 100 for 1961–65. Linking the 1970 index to the 1952–56 base by means of the 1969 index indicates the 1970 index in terms of the 1952–56 base is 113.08. The index for the 1961–65 base was 100 for 1965, and 105 for 1970. Almost all the increase came from the developed world; over the last five or ten years almost no gain has been achieved in the less-developed countries.

[14] The index for per capita total agricultural production was 101 in 1955 and 110 in 1969 on the base period 1952–56; it was 100 in 1965, 103 in 1969 and 103 in 1970 with the base period 1961–65. The slower growth in this index is perhaps partly due to the increase in artificial substitutes for nonfood crops such as synthetic fibers.

[15] FAO *Production Yearbook*, for 1956, 1966, and 1971. Arable land also includes land under permanent crops (orchards, etc.). The totals were 1.370 billion ha. in 1955, 1.428 for 1965, and 1.432 for 1970.

[16] FAO, *Production Yearbook: 1971*, pp. 705–706.

[17] For example, if total agricultural output per hectare increased 2.49 percent per year, then the 2.7 rule would indicate that fertilizer use should increase 6.73 percent per year (see the first two entries for "Total agricultural output per hectare"). The calculations were based on the exponential forms rather than the discrete formulations. If we let O be the total agricultural output per hectare, then $O = k_1 e^{yt}$ where k_1 is a constant, y is the annual growth rate, and t is time. The amount of fertilizer needed according to the 2.7 rule is $F = k_2 O^{2.7}$, where k_2 is a constant, or $F = (k_2) \cdot (k_1)^{2.7} (e^{yt})^{2.7} = k_3 e^{(2.7y)t}$, where k_3 is a constant equal to $(k_2) \cdot (k_1)^{2.7}$. The annual exponential growth rate is then $2.7 \times y$. For our example above, y was 2.49 percent and $2.7 \times y = 6.73$ percent. It should be noted that the

exponential form was also used to calculate the 2.7 rule predictions based on world population, and that all growth rates in parentheses in Table B-1 were also exponential annual growth rates. These give answers approximately equal to the discrete forms (which lend themselves to explanation better than the exponential forms) but are easier to work with than the discrete forms.

[18] Again, these were computed from exponential growth rates. Total annual usage of fertilizer, R, is equal to F, the amount used per hectare, times L, the amount of arable land. From the previous footnote, $F = k_3 \times e^{(2.7y)t}$. If land is growing at exponential annual rate z, then $L = L_o e^{zt}$, where L_o is a constant. Substituting, we find that $R = F \cdot L$, or $R = (k_3) \cdot (L_o) \cdot (e^{(2.7y)t}) \cdot (e^{zt}) = (k_4) \cdot e^{(2.7y+z)t}$, where k_4 is just k_3 times L_o. From this formulation the predicted (by the 2.7 rule) increase in annual worldwide fertilizer use is $2.7y + z$. Therefore, to reflect the increase of arable land on predicted fertilizer usage it is merely necessary to add the exponential growth rate for arable land (z) to the predicted growth rate for fertilizer usage per hectare ($2.7y$). For example, if the predicted fertilizer growth rate per hectare based on total agricultural output per hectare is 6.73 percent per year, and if the annual exponential growth rate of arable land over the same period is 0.56 percent, then the predicted annual growth rate of rate for total use of fertilizer is 6.73 + 0.56, or 7.29 percent.

[19] Straight-line projections of fertilizer use might be just as accurate for short-period predictions.

Appendix C:
Individual Country
Comparisons

This appendix contains the analysis, referred to in Chapter 3, concerning phosphate fertilizer usage in certain countries with high population densities per arable hectare. In this analysis the actual usage of phosphate fertilizer is contrasted with the usage predicted by the 2.7 rule and the FAO formula.

The entries in Table C–1 are intended to summarize the comparative analysis of actual and predicted phosphorus fertilizer usage in the countries indicated there. Countries with relatively large ratios of people per arable hectare were chosen for examination since these countries will probably be more reflective of future conditions when the world population is expected to be much larger. In addition, it is large world populations which present the threat of ultimate P exhaustion.

Fertilizer Usage Calculations

The first column of Table C–1 represents the average amount of P contained in fertilizer applied per hectare of arable land in each country listed. The usage of P_2O_5 as fertilizer (including direct applications of ground phosphate rock and guano), both in total and for each country, was taken from the FAO's *Fertilizers* and *Annual Fertilizer Review* for various years. Since the number of persons supported per hectare (column 2) was derived in two or three different ways, the total

TABLE C-1. Comparisons of the Phosphorus (P) Fertilizer Predictions from the 2.7 Rule and the FAO Equation with Individual Country Data

Country	Actual P fertilizer usage (kg./arable hectare/year) (1)	Number of persons supported per arable hectare (2)	Actual P fertilizer usage per person supported (kg./capita/ year) (3)	Direct and indirect calories consumed per capita: Per day (4)	Per year (10⁶) (5)	Calories produced (10⁶ calories/ arable hectare/year) (Col. 2 × Col. 5) (6)
Haiti	0.6	9.9	0.07	1,930	0.70	7.0
Indonesia	1.4	8.5	0.16	1,760	0.64	5.4
China	1.7	6.8	0.25	2,130	0.78	5.3
Peru	2.7	5.0	0.64	2,330	0.85	4.2
Kenya	4.0	6.7	0.58	2,170	0.79	5.3
United Arab Republic	7.1	10.1	0.72	2,970	1.09	11.0
Taiwan	20.0	14.0	1.4	2,790	1.02	14.3
South Korea	24.0	11.3	2.1	2,380	0.87	9.8
Netherlands	51.0	7.6	6.8	4,500	1.64	12.5
Japan	54.0	8.5	6.6	3,990	1.46	12.4

fertilizer usage was averaged for each of these different calculations. That is, if one method used for a country was based on 1967 data and a second method for the same country was based on an average of 1965–68 data, then the figures for total P fertilizer usage in that country for 1967 and 1965–68 were averaged.

To obtain the annual per hectare usage for each country, the total amount of P fertilizer was divided by the total arable land figure for the corresponding year, given in various yearly issues of the FAO *Production Yearbook* (Table 1). The figure for land under permanent crops was added to the arable land figure since such land (orchards, etc.) often receives fertilizer applications.

Self-Sufficiency Calculations

The number in column 2 multiplied by the arable hectares in each country will in general not equal the population of that country be-

Persons supportable per hectare at 1.5×10^6 calories/year (Col. 6 ÷ 1.5) (7)	World population (billions) at support level in:		Predicted levels of P fertilizer use (kg./arable hectare/year) for population indicated in:			
	Column 2 (Col. 2 × 1.424) (8)	Column 7 (Col. 7 × 1.424) (9)	Column 8 Predicted by:		Column 9 Predicted by:	
			2.7 rule (10)	FAO formula (11)	2.7 rule (12)	FAO formula (13)
4.6	14.1	6.6	210	130	28	31
3.6	12.0	5.2	140	100	14	18
3.6	9.7	5.1	78	68	13	17
2.8	7.1	4.0	33	36	7	9
3.5	9.5	5.0	74	66	13	17
7.3	14.4	10.4	230	140	95	78
9.5	19.9	13.5	540	220	190	120
6.5	16.0	9.3	300	160	69	62
8.3	10.8	11.8	100	82	130	97
8.2	12.1	11.7	140	100	130	95

cause of imports and exports of food, feed, and other crops, and because of fish consumed. For example, if a country imported half of its agricultural crops, exported none, and consumed no fish, then multiplying the number in column 2 by the arable hectares in that country would yield a population equal to half the actual population.

For most countries three methods were employed to calculate the number of persons supported per arable hectare. One method was based on dollar values of crop production, exports, imports, and fish consumed.[1] Essentially, for each country, an attempt was made to value domestic crop production in some set of consistent domestic prices, then add imports of crops (as well as the crops used to produce meat and livestock products, and the crops that would be necessary to produce the equivalent meat for fish imports) valued in the same prices, subtract exports of crops (with similar treatment of meat, livestock and fish products) valued in these same prices, and then add the crop equivalent of fish consumed, again valued in the same prices.

This calculation provided a dollar estimate of domestic consumption, which was divided by the value of domestic crop production (also valued in the same domestic prices) to determine a "self-sufficiency" ratio for each country (where the data allowed this).

The population of the country (from the UN's *Demographic Year-book* series, the FAO's *Production Yearbook* and other sources) was divided by the number of arable hectares to obtain the number of people per arable hectare. This in turn was multiplied by the self-sufficiency ratio to estimate the number of people who might be supported by each arable hectare. Also, the P fertilizer and arable land estimates for the same approximate date as the crop production data were chosen. In most cases this date was 1968 or 1969 because of lack of complete production and trade data for later periods.

A second approach to calculating the number of people that could be supported by each domestic arable hectare in each country was through "food balance" data (again, for those countries where data were available). The calculations and corrections for imports, exports, and fish were essentially the same as those for the dollar valuation method, except that calories instead of dollars were used as the weighting factors. That is, domestic consumption of calories (including the indirect calories consumed by animals and the animal equivalent of fish in feed crops, and excluding the calories in meat, livestock products and fish directly consumed) was divided by domestic production of crop calories to obtain another estimate of the self-sufficiency ratio, which, in turn, led to another estimate of the number of people supported per arable hectare. The prime data sources for these estimates were the FAO's *Food Balance Sheets: 1964–1966* (published in 1971) and the Organization for Economic Co-operation and Development's (OECD) *Food Consumption Statistics: 1960–1968*. Again, phosphate fertilizer and arable land estimates for the corresponding dates were chosen.

The third method of estimating the number of people that could be supported by each arable hectare was that based on actual production data from the sources listed above (primarily the FAO's *Production Yearbook* series). The number of calories produced from crops for some particular year (usually 1969) was divided by the arable land to estimate the calorie production per hectare per year. This estimate was adjusted to allow for losses in processing, based on information contained in the two references concerning food balances listed in the previous paragraph, and from Charlotte Chatfield, *Food Composition Tables for International Use* (FAO, October 1949) and Bernice K. Watt and Annabel L. Merrill of USDA, *Composition of Foods: Raw, Processed and Prepared*, Agricultural Handbook No. 8 (Government Printing Office, December 1963). The estimate of adjusted annual calories per hectare was then divided by the corresponding annual per capita direct and indirect calorie consumption (entered in columns 4 and 5 of Table C–1) derived from the food balance approach. The result of this division provided a third estimate of the number of persons that could be supported on each hectare in each country.

The number of persons supported per arable hectare, in column 2 of Table C–1, was the average of the two or three calculations made for each country. Similarly, the number in column 1 for the actual annual P fertilizer use per arable hectare was the average of the usage rates associated with each of the two or three calculation methods employed. Column 3 is the amount of kilograms of P as fertilizer used annually per person supported. It is roughly equal to the number in column 1 divided by the associated number in column 2. However, the number in column 3 does not exactly equal column 1 divided by column 2 because it was derived by averaging the individual results from each of the two or three calculations.

Calculation Details and Calculation Estimate Deficiencies. It is obvious, of course, that there are many theoretical and practical shortcomings of these three approaches to measuring the number of people each hectare in various countries might support. For instance, the data are often suspect. Weights such as calories or dollars may not be very good ones. Reasonable dollar valuations are difficult where highly processed foods (e.g., candy or prepared cereals) are involved. It has been suggested that instead of using calories, protein content would have been a better measure.[2] In most of these calculations non-food crops such as cotton, tobacco, and timber have not been counted very well, if at all. These and other deficiencies bring into question the validity of the results.

Partly because of this but also because this entire analysis of individual countries has not—contrary to our initial expectations—plàyed a very important part in the overall presentation, the underlying details of these calculations are not provided. To provide them, or even a sample, would require an amount of writing and time that would be greatly out of proportion to their worth. Also, the number of pages involved would lend them an importance that is not justified.[3]

Calorie Production and Consumption Estimates

The data in columns 4 and 5 of Table C-1 are the average per capita daily and annual calories consumed in each country during the 1964–66 period (1968–69 for Japan and the Netherlands) as derived from the food balance calculations described above. These figures exclude calories lost in processing to edible forms and calories consumed in the form of meat, eggs, and dairy products eaten directly; they include instead the caloric content of crop feed given to animals. This adjustment was deemed necessary to reflect the fact that it is crop feed which requires P fertilizer, not animals (although a minor amount of P is used as a feed supplement). Not only were the caloric values of imported food and feed crops included but also an equivalent feed crop adjustment for imports of meat and for consumption of fish. On the other hand, the caloric content of industrial crops such as cotton and timber was not included.

For most of the less-developed countries these adjustments are small, since small amounts of fish and animal products are consumed and some animals survive by grazing on nonarable land. However, for the other countries the adjustment is larger. For example, standard sources indicate the average daily input of calories in the Netherlands is about 3,200, whereas inclusion of feed and feed equivalents in places of meat and fish products increases this to 4,500 calories.

Column 6 is the estimated annual number of calories produced per arable hectare (on which food crops are grown). It is the product of column 2 (the number of people supported per arable hectare) and column 5 (the per capita annual calorie consumption). A direct calculation of this estimate was performed, as outlined above, to obtain an estimate of the number of persons supported per arable hectare for column 2, and the differences between these direct production estimates and those in column 6 are within tolerable limits.

Since the per capita caloric values for many of the less-developed countries seem fairly inadequate, and may really be much higher than reported statistics indicate, it was assumed that all countries are consuming, or may consume within some period of time, about 1.5 million calories per person per year (4,110 calories per day). The number of persons supportable per hectare at this level of calorie consumption was calculated by dividing column 6 by 1.5. This is recorded in column 7.

Comparison with the 2.7 Rule and FAO Formula Predictions

Given any number of persons supportable per arable hectare in column 2, it is possible to calculate from the 2.7 rule or the modified FAO formula what level of fertilizer use should be necessary to support that number of people from crops grown on one hectare of arable land at the world average calorie consumption level. For the less-developed countries, the actual calorie consumption level is below the world average, so biases in the results are present. Reverse biases are present for the more developed countries. To offset these biases, population densities at consumption levels that are probably well above average (shown in column 7) have also been used in the two formulas for the calculation of fertilizer "requirements."

In order to obtain these fertilizer requirements from either formula it is necessary to calculate the world population at the given population density per arable hectare. Thus, for China, if a population of 6.8 persons per arable hectare could be established on every arable hectare in the world (1,424 million ha.), the world population supportable at the Chinese fertilizer rate of 1.7 kg. of P per hectare would be 9.7 billion people (column 8).

From the 2.7 rule the annual world use of P in fertilizer for a population of 9.7 billion would be 112 million metric tons (not shown in Table C–1) or 78 kg. of P per arable hectare (column 10 for China). This last figure is to be compared with the actual P fertilizer use in China of 1.7 kg. per arable hectare (column 1).

Similarly, based on this same world population of 9.7 billion, it is possible from the modified FAO equation to calculate, as in Table 3, the world fertilizer usage. The world use of P as fertilizer from the modified FAO formula in this example is an estimated 97 million tons per year, or 68 kg. per arable hectare (column 11 for China).[4]

But, as already noted, it is implicit in these two calculations that a population of 9.7 billion could be supported at the average Chinese calorie consumption level. However, the world average daily per capita direct and indirect crop calorie intake is higher than 2,100 calories. At a higher level of consumption, a level even higher than the present world average level, only about 3.6 people (column 7) could be supported per arable hectare in China. If this support level were possible on all arable land in the world, the world population could only be 5.1 billion (column 9) instead of 9.7 billion. Based on a population of 5.1 billion, 13 kg. of P per arable hectare per year would be used according to the 2.7 rule (column 12) and 17 kg. per arable hectare per year according to the modified FAO formula (column 13). The "correct" predictions for each formula probably lie somewhere between the entries in columns 10 and 11, on the one hand, and 12 and 13, on the other.

Despite the fact that the data and methods are crude, it is apparent that in comparison with actual P fertilizer dosages, in every case the two formulas overestimate the amount of phosphorus fertilizer needed, and the amount of overestimate is significantly worse in absolute terms for the countries with high output per hectare. Also in these cases, the 2.7 rule yields even higher estimates than the FAO formula. The overestimates are in part due to the deliberate selection of countries with high numbers of people per arable hectare. But, of course, it is just these countries which are of most interest. If the two formulas fail to reflect fertilizer use very well in these countries, then serious doubts can be cast upon them, since higher world population densities are to be expected as population rises. The formulas may be quite acceptable for predictive purposes in lower density countries but this is of little interest here.

Both the UAR and Taiwan deserve special mention. The UAR is somewhat anomalous because, before the completion of the Aswan Dam, the Nile brought much of the plant nutrients to the fields. Without this source of nutrients, processed fertilizer usage would have to be increased, or yields would decline. As indicated in Chapter 3, the huge disparity between the formula predictions of fertilizer usage and the actual rate in Taiwan is probably due mainly to double and triple cropping there.[5]

Notes

[1] The physical production data were taken from sources such as the FAO's annual *Production Yearbook* and the publications of the Foreign Regional Analysis Division of the U.S. Department of Agriculture's Economic Research Service, entitled *Indices of Agricultural Production,* for various world regions. Import and export information came from various annual editions of the FAO's *Trade Yearbook,* the United Nations' *Commodity Trade Statistics* and *Foreign Trade Statistics for Africa,* and the Foreign Regional Analysis Division's (of USDA's Economic Research Service) *Agricultural Trade of the Western Hemisphere.* Fish consumption data were taken from the FAO's *Yearbook of Fishery Statistics.*

[2] By letter communication, Professor Frederick E. Smith, who participated in preparing the TIE report, points out that "The correlation of P and calories in foods is not good, even among grains alone. . . . P is linked to protein, not to calories, and . . . [the] analysis should be based on protein consumption, not calorie consumption." Time limitations have prevented such an analysis, but allowances have been made for higher levels of phosphorus intake (via animal feed) in developing the 10-to-20 kg. of P per capita per year rule discussed in Chapter 3.

[3] One matter which might be mentioned here is that a disproportionate amount of time was spent in making these calculations for column 2 because of lack of data, and, more importantly, because of the lack of clarity in the existing and available data. It would be most useful to have a guide to agricultural statistics so that a researcher not familiar with the field could find out what is available, what the statistics mean, and how they should be interpreted.

[4] For all the 2.7 rule and the FAO equation estimations in columns 10 through 13, the 1968 base usage of 7.6 million metric tons of P in fertilizer was used in place of 1968 total production of 11.3 million metric tons of P for all uses, because the 7.6 million tons refers to fertilizer applied and is hence more directly comparable to the figure indicated in column 1 of Table C-1.

[5] Each crop yielded only about 10 million calories per hectare (slightly below the Japanese and Netherlands levels) but because of multiple cropping, the annual yield was raised to about 18 million calories per hectare. These figures are taken from the direct output calculations discussed above and, therefore, do not agree with the data in column 6 of Table C-1.

The production data indicate that about 1.8 crops per hectare per year were grown in Taiwan on average. This agrees fairly well with the figures reported by Dana G. Dalrymple, *Survey of Multiple Cropping in Less Developed Nations*, FEDR-12 (Washington: Foreign Economic Development Service, U.S. Department of Agriculture, October 1971), pp. 90–93. Dalrymple estimates that about 1.8 to 1.9 crops are grown on the average arable hectare in each year.

Appendix D:
Erosion Control
and Soil Fixation

In developing the estimate of 10–20 kg. of phosphorus per capita annual physical requirements for crops in Chapter 3, it is stated that phosphorus losses of two sorts must be considered. The first one is the loss of phosphorus by soil erosion. The second is the chemical "fixation" of phosphorus within the soil so that the phosphorus becomes "unavailable" for plant growth. For this 10 to 20 kg. rule to hold, most such losses must be prevented. In Appendix D both soil erosion and soil fixation losses of P are examined.

Erosion Losses of Phosphorus

Most phosphate fertilizer leaves the soil in crops or through soil erosion and water runoff.[1] It is almost universally held that very little P is lost from water percolating down through the soil or leaching.[2] Measurements of the amounts of P lost from the soil by water erosion and runoff can vary significantly from almost no loss to over 50 kg. per hectare, with loss rates evidently dependent on erosion and runoff rates.[3]

Soil conservation has long been of concern, and numerous control methods have been developed. These include various forms of vegetative cover; tillage, planting and cultivation practices, terracing, contouring, reservoirs, soil stabilization structures, and others. It is claimed that erosion control measures can reduce existing soil losses in this country by 75 percent and more.[4]

However, it is argued that reduction of soil erosion by any given amount such as 75 percent might not be accompanied by a proportionate reduction in phosphate loss.[5] Since almost all of the fertilizer P attaches to the soil near the point of application, which is usually on the top of the soil, even slight erosion removes the significant amounts of P contained in the topmost soil. One solution would be to apply the phosphate fertilizer slightly below the surface—a practice which is held beneficial for crops in any event[6] and also helps avoid quick run-off losses of P from heavy rains occurring before the P becomes attached to the soil or absorbed by crop plants.

Costs of Reducing Erosion.   Although soil loss rates vary considerably depending upon rainfall, climate, soil type, land slope, crops, control measures, and other factors, consideration of a particular study may be helpful.[7] In this study a drainage area (the Nishnabotna River Basin) of 2,800 square miles (7,300 km.²) in southwestern Iowa within the Missouri River Basin was evaluated. This area is characterized by high productivity but also high erodability. For cropped areas, Seay considers conventional tillage, an alternative "no-plow" minimum tillage,[8] with or without contouring, and with or without terracing.

Without any erosion control measures, conventional tillage for a corn–corn–soybean crop rotation over three years results in average annual soil losses ranging from an estimated 12 tons per hectare to 400 tons per hectare depending upon the degree of slope and average length of slope involved. Minimum tillage alone is estimated to reduce these erosion rates by about one-half.[9] Since the costs of conventional tillage to the farmer are 40 percent higher than those of minimum tillage, minimum tillage clearly dominates conventional tillage (and minimum tillage methods are now being widely adopted throughout the country).

Contouring in association with minimum tillage is estimated by Seay to increase yearly production costs $6 per hectare, from $47 per hectare (minimum tillage alone) to $53 per hectare per year and to cut erosion, depending on the land slope gradient, by an additional 40 to 50 percent over minimum tillage without contouring. In contrast to minimum tillage alone, combining terracing with minimum tillage reduces soil erosion by over 97 percent (in comparison with minimum tillage alone) and increases costs, including costs due to production foregone from terracing, by between $18 per hectare and $36 per hectare per year over those of minimum tillage alone.

Tentative Cost Estimates of Reducing Phosphate Erosion Losses.   If we set aside the objections of Aldrich et al. concerning the fact that minimum tillage and other soil conservation measures may not reduce phosphorus loss in the same proportion as the reduction in soil loss, it is then possible to calculate the costs of preventing the loss of P off the land into possibly more dilute environments. Assuming on average that the phosphorus content of soils is about 0.1 percent,[10] the estimated loss of P per hectare per year would range, depending on ground slope, between 6 and 190 kg. for crop land under minimum tillage alone in the area Seay examined. Considering the amount of crop land in each grade-slope category, the annual average would be about 54 kg. per hectare.

Terracing plus minimum tillage would result in an estimated annual P loss of between 0.4 and 2.7 kg. per hectare, or an average of about 0.9 kg. per hectare in the cropped area. If the annual saving due to the introduction of terracing is 53 kg. of P per hectare at an annual average cost of $27 per hectare (again weighted by the amount of crop land in each grade-slope class), the cost per metric ton of P saved would be approximately $500.

Not only because of the objections raised by Aldrich et al., but also because the potential soil loss in the region studied by Seay is greater than most areas, the actual average cost of avoiding P losses off the land might be several times as much as $500 per ton.[11] Against this, however, the costs of extracting P from common rocks at a cost of $11,000 per ton must be considered. The P in the soil is already on the farmers' land while P extracted from rock must be processed into fertilizer and delivered, and the price of P delivered to the U.S. farmer is, as noted in a previous section, about $420 per metric ton.[12]

In addition, soil conservation does have other benefits. It saves the soil for the farmer and reduces the amount of phosphate, nitrogen, pesticides, organic matter and soil sediment reaching streams. Currently there is much concern over the possibility that phosphates and nitrogen introduced into various water bodies may be accelerating their eutrophication, and measures to reduce the input of these and other sediment-associated pollutants may be implemented in any event. Finally, improvements in technology and techniques such as recirculation of agricultural runoff water might reduce costs.

Soil Fixation

If, in fact, losses of P from erosion and runoff can be controlled, there is still the question of the availability of the P retained in the soil. The reason leaching or deep percolation losses of P are so small is that most of the phosphate becomes chemically "fixed" to the soil.[13] Phosphate which is fixed may be unavailable or only slowly available to crops.[14]

A number of studies provide useful information on this subject. Vincent Sauchelli reports that "plants on phosphorus-fertilized soils generally recover from 20 to 30 percent of the applied phosphate in the first year and progressively decreasing amounts in succeeding years."[15] He also cites various experiments which show that the residual phosphorus in the soil may increase plant growth for as long as ten or fifteen years after application. McVickar points out that in one experiment the increase in yield (compared with the unfertilized yields) in the fourth year after P fertilization was about 70 percent as great as in the first year after fertilization.[16] Moore et al. and Campbell indicate that recovery rates for an initial application of phosphate fertilizer range between 40 and 70 percent over a period of about ten years (or really ten crops).[17] Ensminger notes significant residual effects remaining twenty years after phosphate fertilizer was stopped in field tests on cotton and other crops.[18]

In reporting much evidence that the phosphate added to soil does not remain permanently fixed or permanently lost to the plants but becomes slowly available over time, Sauchelli argues that the soil is somewhat like a sponge soaking up water, that is, the P is absorbed by the soil until enough has been added, and then all additions become more or less available.[19] Thus, if soil erosion is substantially controlled, the recovery rates of P by crops would likely be quite high over periods of thirty or fifty years. Inasmuch as periods of hundreds and thousands of years are being examined, it seems reasonable to assume fairly high-level percentage recovery rates. In any event, it appears that up to a certain point adding phosphate in a more water-soluble or available state helps decrease fixation.[20] Reduction of soil acidity (through application of lime, for example) also helps "unlock" phosphates fixed in the soil (probably in part because few vigorous crop plants grow well on acid soils).

In the long run it is perhaps not unreasonable to expect that ways will be found to increase the efficiency with which plants make use of phosphorus in the soil. It is also possible that improvements in packaging and other methods might be found to decrease soil fixation. For example, one possibility is to encase the phosphorus fertilizer in biodegradable plastic packages which would release the soluble phosphorus slowly over time at the rate plant growth dictates.[21]

With respect to soil erosion, fixation and other losses, Ensminger has commented:

Added phosphorus accumulates to some extent in soils. This occurs because only a small percentage of phosphorus applied in fertilizers is removed in the harvested portion of crops or lost by leaching. Extent of accumulation depends on such factors as amount of phosphorus added, amount lost by erosion, crop grown, and how much of the crop is removed from the land. . . . Loss of phosphorus by erosion and runoff has been recognized as an important factor in reducing the accumulation of applied phosphates. . . . Chemical fixation of phosphorus by soils has been credited with the low-efficiency [i.e., low initial recovery percentage] often obtained. Fixation, which is the reversion to a less [water] soluble form, is undoubtedly responsible for some loss in availability of phosphorus. However, yield data and radiophosphorus uptake [by plants] have shown that fixed phosphorus is fairly available to plants.[22]

Ensminger's results indicate that phosphate recovery by plants from any single dose does indeed take a number of years but that the phosphate is not permanently lost if erosion control is practiced.

Notes

[1] In this connection it is claimed that wind erosion losses are usually insignificant, although, in particular places, under adverse conditions they can be serious. In the U.S. each year, according to Alexander, about 30 million tons of dust, much of it from the soil, enters the atmosphere in contrast to about 4,000 million tons of soil sediment entering waterways and reservoirs. See M. Alexander, "Environmental Consequences of Rapidly Rising Food Output," a paper presented at the Columbia/United Nations Conference on Development and the Environment (December 2, 1971), pp. 14–15. Also, Combined Report by Canada and the United States for the Environmental Protection Agency, *Agricultural Pollution of the Great Lakes Basin* (July 1, 1971), Part B, p. 26.

[2] C. A. Black, "Behavior of Soil and Fertilizer Phosphorus in Relation to Water Pollution," in Ted L. Willrich and George E. Smith, eds., *Agricultural Practices and Water Quality* (Ames, Iowa: The Iowa State University Press, 1970), pp. 72–93; W. P. Martin, W. F. Fenster, and L. D. Hanson, "Fertilizer Management for Pollution Control," ibid., pp. 146–147; and D. E. Armstrong and G. A. Rohlich, "Effects of Agricultural Pollution on Eutrophication," ibid., pp. 316–319.

[3] Armstrong and Rohlich, ibid., pp. 319–325.

[4] Martin et al., ibid., p. 145.

[5] S. R. Aldrich, W. R. Oschwald, and J. B. Fehrenbacher, "Implications of Crop-Production Technology for Environmental Quality," in Robert E. Bergstrom, ed., *Land Use Problems in Illinois*, Environmental Geology Notes of the Illinois State Geological Survey, no. 46 (May 1971), p. 15.

[6] Malcolm H. McVickar, *Using Commercial Fertilizers: Commercial Fertilizers and Crop Production* (3rd ed., Danville, Illinois: Interstate Printers and Publishers, Inc., 1970), pp. 181–197.

[7] Edmond E. Seay, Jr., *Minimizing Abatement Costs of Water Pollutants from Agriculture: A Parametric Linear Programming Approach*, Preliminary Report (Ames, Iowa: Department of Economics of Iowa State University, 1970). Most of the information cited here is contained in Chapter 4, Appendix A, and Appendix B.

[8] No-plow tillage involves leaving the nonedible portions of the crops on the field and replanting without plowing. The elimination of plowing and the covering of the soil by plant residues substantially reduce soil erosion mainly because, to the extent the soil is covered by plant residues, it is protected from rain.

[9] Even higher rates of soil erosion reduction from minimum tillage have been reported. See John K. Maddy, "Crop Residues Substitute for Grass in Rotation," *Soil Conservation*, vol. 35, no. 1 (August 1969), p. 8.

However, Aldrich et al. ("Implications of Crop-Production Technology," p. 15) argue that minimum tillage may not be very effective in reducing the loss of phosphorus because "when plant residues decay on the soil surface, the resulting soluble organic phosphorus compounds are readily carried into streams and lakes, especially when the soil is frozen."

[10] C. A. Black, "Behavior of Soil and Fertilizer Phosphorus in Relation to Water Pollution," pp. 89–90; W. P. Martin, W. F. Fenster and L. D. Hanson, "Fertilizer Management for Pollution Control," p. 146; D. E. Armstrong and G. A. Rohlich, *Management of Nutrients on Agricultural Land for Improved Water Quality* (Ithaca, N.Y.: Department of Agronomy, Cornell University, 1971), p. 316, figures 5, 8, 13, 16, 19, and 24; and G. Stanford, C. B. England, and A. W. Taylor, *Fertilizer Use and Water Quality*, U.S. Department of Agriculture, Agricultural Research Service Publication 41-168 (October 1970), p. 17.

[11] On the other hand, not all the P eroded soil ends up in a lake or ocean. Perhaps one-half or so (Seay, *Minimizing Abatement Costs*, p. 75) is deposited on other land before reaching the stream, river, or other body of water. Some of the P deposited on other land might contribute to that land's fertility.

[12] This argument overlooks the fact that the P saved from erosion may be much less "available" to crops than the P applied by way of fertilizer. It also tends to suggest that the best thing to do in the long run is to allow erosion of soils depleted of P by successive cropping, and then crop the lower less-depleted soils. If the soil contains 0.1 percent P, then why not just crop it instead of mining a rock ore of the same level of P content? The trouble here is that eventually no topsoil would be left. However, in the extreme and unlikely event that it is necessary to extract P from common rock, it might be cheaper to attempt to crush and convert the rock into a proper growth medium and allow the plants to extract the P rather than directly attempting to remove it.

[13] I am particularly indebted to Gilbert L. Terman of the Soils and Fertilizer Research Branch of the Tennessee Valley Authority's Division of Agricultural Development at Muscle Shoals, Alabama, for references and suggestions concerning this topic.

[14] Fixation of P evidently varies greatly by kind of soil as well.

[15] Vincent Sauchelli, *Phosphates in Agriculture* (2nd ed., New York: Reinhold, 1965), p. 78.

According to Terman (letter communication), D. G. Moore, O. J. Attoe, and C. I. Rich ("Recovery by Eleven Crops of Oats of Phosphorus Applied to Pot Cultures of Five Soils," *Agronomy Journal*, vol. 49 (1957), pp. 560–563) report similar results for the first crop recovery of phosphorus fertilizer.

[16] McVickar, *Using Commercial Fertilizers*, p. 63. Sauchelli also reports on results falling in this range (*Phosphates in Agriculture*, pp. 173–174).

[17] Moore et al., "Recovery by Eleven Crops of Oats"; and R. E. Campbell, "Phosphorus Fertilizer Residual Effects on Irrigated Crops in Rotation," *Soil Science Society of America Proceedings*, vol. 29 (1965), pp. 67–70, as cited by Terman.

[18] L. E. Ensminger, *Residual Value of Phosphates*, Auburn University Agricultural Experiment Station Bulletin 322 (January 1960), Figure 1, p. 5. At least for these particular crops and soils it appears that the residual effects would be measurable for quite a while longer since at the end of the twenty years the yields from the initially fertilized fields were still significantly higher than the yields from the unfertilized check plots.

[19] Sauchelli, *Phosphates in Agriculture*, Chapter 7. He also suggests that soil erosion losses of P may account for some experimental work indicating that part of the residual P never becomes available to the plants and is therefore, essentially, lost forever (p. 172).

[20] Some phosphate rock is directly applied as a fertilizer material without further processing. However, the phosphorus in phosphate rock is not very soluble and so is even less available for plant growth. Therefore, very little phosphate rock is used directly.

[21] This paragraph is based on suggestions provided by Arnold C. Orvedal.

[22] Ensminger, *Residual Value of Phosphates*, pp. 3–4.

Selected Bibliography

BARNETT, HAROLD J., and MORSE, CHANDLER. *Scarcity and Growth: The Economics of Natural Resource Availability.* Baltimore: Johns Hopkins University Press, 1963.

BRADFIELD, RICHARD. "Training Agronomists for Increasing Food Production in the Humid Tropics," in J. Ritchie Cowan and L. S. Robertson, eds., *International Agronomy: Training and Education,* ASA Special Publication Number 15. Madison, Wisconsin: American Society of Agronomy, 1969.

BROWN, HARRISON. *The Challenge of Man's Future: An Inquiry Concerning the Condition of Man During the Years That Lie Ahead.* New York: Viking Press, 1954.

BROWN, K. B. "Recovery of Phosphate Fertilizer from Ordinary Igneous Rock." Memo. Oak Ridge, Tennessee: Oak Ridge National Laboratory, September 13, 1971.

CHATFIELD, CHARLOTTE. *Food Composition Tables for International Use.* Washington, D.C.: Food and Agriculture Organization of the United Nations, October 1949.

DALRYMPLE, DANA G. *Controlled Environmental Agriculture: A Global Review of Greenhouse Food Production.* Foreign Agricultural Economic Report No. 89 of the Economic Research Service of the U.S. Department of Agriculture. Washington, D.C.: Government Printing Office, 1973.

DE WIT, C. T. "Food Production: Past, Present, and Future," *Stikstof* No. 15 (January 1972).

EMIGH, G. DONALD. "World Phosphate Reserves—Are There Really Enough?" *Engineering and Mining Journal,* April 1972.

ENNIS, W. B., JR., JANSEN, L. L., ELLIS, I. J., and NEWSOM, L. D. "Inputs for Pesticides," *The World Food Problem,* Panel on the World Food Supply of the President's Science Advisory Committee, Vol. III. Washington, D.C.: Government Printing Office, 1967.

114

ENSMINGER, L. E. *Residual Value of Phosphates*, Bulletin 322. Auburn, Alabama: Auburn University Agricultural Experiment Station, January, 1960.

FOOD AND AGRICULTURE ORGANIZATION OF THE UNITED NATIONS. *Annual Fertilizer Review: 1970*. Rome: FAO, 1971.

————. *Fertilizers: An Annual Review of World Production, Consumption and Trade* (Annual editions prior to 1970). Rome: FAO.

————. *Food Balance Sheets: 1964–1966*. Rome: FAO, 1971.

————. *Production Yearbook* (Annual editions). Rome: FAO.

————. *Trade Yearbook* (Annual editions). Rome: FAO.

————. *Yearbook of Fishery Statistics* (Annual editions). Rome: FAO.

IGNATIEFF, VLADIMIR, and PAGE, HAROLD J., eds. *Efficient Use of Fertilizers*. FAO Agricultural Studies No. 43. Rome: revised ed., FAO, 1958.

KELLOGG, CHARLES E., and ORVEDAL, ARNOLD C. "Potentially Arable Soils of the World and Critical Measures for Their Use," *Advances in Agronomy*, vol. 21 (1969).

LEWIS, RICHARD W. "Phosphorus," *Mineral Facts and Problems*. U.S. Bureau of Mines Bulletin 650. Washington, D.C.: Government Printing Office, 1970.

LOVERING, THOMAS S. "Mineral Resources from the Land," *Resources and Man*, Committee on Resources and Man of the Division of Earth Sciences, National Academy of Sciences—National Research Council. San Francisco: W. H. Freeman and Company, 1969.

MCKELVEY, V. E. "Mineral Resource Estimates and Public Policy," in Donald A. Probst and Walden P. Pratt, eds., *United States Mineral Resources*, Geological Survey Professional Paper 820. Washington, D.C.: Government Printing Office, 1973.

————. *Phosphate Deposits*, U.S. Geological Survey Bulletin 1252-D. Washington, D.C.: Government Printing Office, 1967.

MCVICKAR, MALCOLM H. *Using Commercial Fertilizers: Commercial Fertilizers and Crop Production*. Danville, Illinois: 3rd ed., Interstate Printers and Publishers, Inc., 1970.

MEADOWS, DONELLA H. et al. *The Limits to Growth*. New York: Universe Books, 1972.

NELSON, LEWIS B., and EWELL, RAYMOND H. "Fertilizer Requirements for Increased Food Needs," *The World Food Problem*, Panel on the World Food Supply of the President's Science Advisory Committee, vol. III. Washington, D.C.: Government Printing Office, 1967.

ORGANIZATION FOR ECONOMIC CO-OPERATION AND DEVELOPMENT. *Food Consumption Statistics: 1960–1968.* Paris: OECD, 1970.

PIRIE, N. W. *Food Resources: Conventional and Novel.* Baltimore: Penguin Books, 1969.

SAUCHELLI, VINCENT. *Phosphates in Agriculture.* New York: 2nd ed., Reinhold, 1965.

SEAY, EDMOND E., JR. *Minimizing Abatement Costs of Water Pollutants from Agriculture: A Parametric Linear Programming Approach, Preliminary Report.* Ames, Iowa: Department of Economics of Iowa State University, 1970. Mimeographed.

SHELDON, RICHARD P. "World Phosphate Resources," *Mining Congress Journal*, vol. 55, no. 2 (February 1969).

TAYLOR, THEODORE B., and HUMPSTONE, CHARLES C. *The Restoration of the Earth.* New York: Harper & Row, 1973.

THE INSTITUTE OF ECOLOGY. *Man in the Living Environment.* Report of the 1971 Workshop on Global Ecological Problems. Chicago: TIE, 1971.

―――. *Man in the Living Environment.* Madison: rev. ed., University of Wisconsin Press, 1972.

UNITED NATIONS, STATISTICAL OFFICE OF THE UN DEPARTMENT OF ECONOMIC AND SOCIAL AFFAIRS, *Commodity Trade Statistics.* (annual) New York.

―――. Economic Commission for Africa. *Foreign Trade Statistics for Africa.* (annual) New York.

UNITED STATES DEPARTMENT OF AGRICULTURE, ECONOMIC RESEARCH SERVICE. *Agricultural Trade of the Western Hemisphere: A Statistical Review.* ERS-Foreign 328. Washington, D.C.: USDA, February 1972.

―――. *Indices of Agricultural Production for East Asia, South Asia, and Oceania: Average 1961–65 and Annual 1962 through 1971.* Washington, D.C.: USDA, April 1972.

————. *Indices of Agricultural Production for the Western Hemisphere, Excluding the United States and Cuba: 1962 through 1971.* ERS-Foreign 264. Washington, D.C.: revised, USDA, March 1972.

————. *Indices of Agricultural Production in Western Europe: 1950–68.* ERS-Foreign 266. Washington, D.C.: USDA, July 1969.

WATT, BERNICE K., and MERRILL, ANNABEL L. *Composition of Foods: Raw, Processed and Prepared.* Agriculture Handbook No. 8, Agricultural Research Service, USDA, Washington, D.C.: revised, Government Printing Office, 1964.

WILLIAMS, MOYLE S., and COUSTON, JOHN W. *Crop Production Levels and Fertilizer Use.* Rome: Food and Agriculture Organization, 1962.

Index

Agricultural production. *See* Crop output
Aldrich, S. R., 54, 57n, 109, 112n
Alexander, M., 112n
Animals, phosphorus concentration in, 54
Armstrong, D. E., 112n
Attoe, O. J., 113n

Barnett, Harold J., 70n
Bergstrom, Robert E., 57n
Black, C. A., 112n
Bradfield, Richard, 37–38, 43n, 44n
Bridger, G. L., 34n
Bromwell, Leslie G., 21n
Brooks, David B., 23n
Brown, Harrison, 21n
Brown, K. B., 6, 7, 22n, 23n
Bureau of Mines, 2, 4
Byerly, T. C., 45n

Calories: conversion ratios, 43n–44n; per capita consumption, 38; production per hectare, 38–39; production under multiple crop experiments, 37; U. S. versus world intake, 44n
Campbell, R. E., 110, 113n
Carlson, Carl, 45n
Cereal grains, production per hectare, 39
Chatfield, Charlotte, 44n
China, fertilizer usage, 30, 34n, 98–99, 104
Cloud, Preston, 16, 23n
Common rock deposits, xv, xvii, 15; amount of phosphorus in, xiv, 5–6; cost of extracting phosphorus from, 42, 61–62, 68, 69, 109, 112n; exhaustion period, 13

Conservation of phosphorus, xiv, xvii, xviii, xixn; by hydroponic greenhouses, 49–52; from synthesizing food, 52; by technological improvements, 48–49, 52; by use of additional land, 47–48
Conservation, soil, 107–08, 109–10
Consumption of phosphorus: per capita, xiii–xiv, 32, 43; population and, xiii–xiv, 2, 5, 20n; TIE estimates of, 1–2, 20n, 62. *See also* Exhaustion of phosphorus; Power rule, 2.7
Continental crustal abundance, 6
Copper, 6–7
Cost of phosphorus: effect of technological improvements on, 18, 24n; in extraction from common rock, 42, 61–62, 68, 69, 109, 112n; in extraction from granite, 6–7, 56; factors contributing to, 85–86; per capita, xvii, xviii, 9–10, 11, 32, 65; saved from erosion, 42
Couston, John W., 27, 34n, 37, 43n
Cowan, J. Ritchie, 43n
Crop output: effect of multicropping on, 36–37; estimates for maximum, 38–40; fertilizer use and, 1, 19n, 27, 88, 91; high-yield, 40–41; index of, per hectare, 94, 97n–98n; per capita, 31, 93, 95n; pesticide use and, 89; yield-value index of, 27–28, 31, 34n

Dalrymple, Dana, 51, 57n
Delson, Jerome K., 22n
Deposits. *See* Reserves
De Wit, C. T., 38–40, 44n, 45n, 48, 57n, 64, 83

Economic deposits, xiv, xv, 2, 4

118

Emigh, G. D., xvii, 20n, 22n, 23n; cost estimates, 7, 18; reserve estimates, 3–5, 12, 19, 60, 68
England, C. B., 112n
Ennis, W. B., 33n, 88, 90, 94n
Ensminger, L. E., 110, 111, 113n
Environmental mining, cost, 8–9
Environmental pollution, from phosphorus, xvi–xvii, 35n
Erosion. *See* Soil erosion; Wind erosion
Ewell, Raymond H., 28, 29, 33n, 34n
Exhaustion of phosphorus: in common rock, 13; under fertilizer consumption assumption, 66–67, 77–83; from modified FAO formula, 31, 32, 77; under 2.7 power rule, 2, 5, 11, 12, 65–66; TIE estimates of, xii, xvii, 10, 60; unlikelihood of, 69

FAO. *See* Food and Agriculture Organization
Fehrenbacher, J. B., 57n, 112n
Fenster, W. F., 45n, 112n
Fertilizer, phosphate: compared with total fertilizer used, 30; consumption based on population, 14, 26, 43, 62; cost, 10, 22n–23n, 46, 66–67, 77–83; effect on crop output, 1, 19n, 27; environmental effect of, 35n; for high-yield agriculture, 40–41; methods of broadcasting, 46; per capita consumption, 42, 66, 98; predicted use of, 36, 98–99; runoff, 9, 41–42; substitution of additional land for, 47–48; use growth rate, 91–92. *See also* Food and Agriculture Organization fertilizer prediction formula
Florida, phosphate wastes, 21n
Food: average U.S. versus world intake, 44n; per capita production, 93, 95n; production per hectare, 39; synthesis, 52, 65, 66
Food and Agriculture Organization (FAO) fertilizer prediction formula, xvii, xviii; application to aggregate data, 29, 32; calculation of, 73–76; compared with 2.7 rule, 27–28, 33, 65–68; modified, 30–31, 42, 65–66; PSAC adaption of, 28; recycling and, 84

Goeller, H. E., 6, 7, 22n
Granite, extraction of phosphorus from, 6–7, 23n, 56
Greenhouses. *See* Hydroponics

Haiti, fertilizer usage, 98–99
Hanson, L. D., 45n, 112n
Humpstone, Charles C., 49, 50, 57n
Hydroponics, 64; cost of, 49–52; explanation of, 49

Ignatieff, Vladimir, 58n
Igneous rock, phosphorus concentration in, 2
India, fertilizer-to-yield relationship, 91
Indonesia, fertilizer usage, 98–99
Institute of Ecology (TIE): estimates of phosphorus reserves, xi, xv, 3, 4, 5, 10–12, 13, 45n, 60; phosphorus consumption estimates, 1–2, 20n; on recycling, 58n. *See also* Power rule, 2.7
International Rice Research Institute, 37

Japan: calorie intake, 102; fertilizer usage, 36, 42, 98–99; fertilizer-to-yield relationship, 91

Kellogg, Charles E., 57n, 94n
Kenya, fertilizer usage, 98–99

Land, arable: available, 47–48, 65, 82–83; changes in, 93, 94
Lasky grade-tonnage ratio, 17–18, 23n
Lasky, S. G., 23n
Leaching, phosphorus loss from, 41, 64, 110
Less-developed regions, fertilizer consumption study, 28–29
Levin, Gilbert V., 58n
Lewis, Richard W., viiin, 20n, 21n, 22n
Lovering, Thomas S., 23n
Low-grade deposits, xiv, xv, 5, 15, 61; Lasky grade-tonnage ratio for, 17–18

McKelvey, V. E., xviii*n*, 16, 18, 23*n*
McVickar, Malcolm H., 34*n*, 45*n*, 58*n*,
  110, 112*n*, 113*n*
Maddy, John K., 112*n*
Manthy, Robert, 70*n*
Manure, recycling phosphorus from,
  64–65
Martin, W. P., 45*n*, 112*n*
Meadows, Dennis L., 70*n*
Meadows, Donella H., 69*n*, 70*n*
Mero, John, 19
Minerals, prices, 70*n*
Mining of phosphorus, 8–9
Moore, D. G., 110, 113*n*
Morse, Chandler, 70*n*
Multiple cropping: Bradfield experi-
  ments with, 37–38; effect on crop
  output, 36–37

Nelson, Lewis B., 28, 29, 33*n*, 34*n*
Nephew, E. A., 22*n*
Netherlands: calorie intake, 102; fer-
  tilizer usage, 36, 42, 98; food pro-
  duction, per hectare, 39
North Korea, fertilizer usage, 30, 34*n*
North Vietnam, fertilizer usage, 30,
  34*n*

Orvedal, Arnold C., 57*n*, 94*n*
Oschwald, W. R., 57*n*, 112*n*

Page, Harold J., 58*n*
Page, Toby, 94*n*
Parker, Frank W., 34*n*
Parker, Raymond L., 21*n*
Peru, fertilizer usage, 98–99
Pesticides: fertilizer usage and, 27,
  33*n*; relation to crop output, 89, 94
Phosphorus: concentration of, 2, 8–9,
  42, 64; crop withdrawal of, 43, 45*n*;
  exploration for, 15–17; loss from
  erosion, 41–42, 43, 53, 107–08; mining
  of, 8–9; solubility of, 21*n*; substitution of other resources for, xi, xiv,
  47–48; units of measure for, xvi;
  uses of, xv–xvi. *See also* Conservation of phosphorus; Cost of phosphorus; Exhaustion of phosphorus;
Phosphorus reserves; Recycling of
  phosphorus
Phosphorus reserves: defined, xi;
  Emigh's estimates of, 3–5, 12, 19, 60,
  68; ocean, 19; supply definitions,
  xiv; TIE estimates of, xi, xv, 3, 4,
  5, 10–12, 13, 45*n*, 60; usable versus
  nonusable, xii, 5, 60–61
Pirie, N. W., 57*n*
Plants: phosphorus concentration in,
  42, 64; withdrawal of phosphorus
  by, 43, 45*n*
Population: density, per hectare, 44*n*–
  45*n*; pattern of growth, 12; phosphorus use and, xiii, xiv, 2, 5, 20*n*,
  32, 43, 91; size limits, 40
Potatoes, production, per hectare, 39
Power rule, 2.7, xvii, xviii, 22*n*; calculation of, 71–73; compared with
  FAO formula, 33, 63, 65–68; estimate of exhaustion time with, 5, 11,
  12, 65–66; explanation of, 1, 25–27,
  88; recycling and, 84; validity of,
  14, 43, 45*n*
President's Science Advisory Committee (PSAC): adaption of FAO
  equation, 28–29, 63; on relation of
  crop output and fertilizer use, 88, 90

Recycling of phosphorus, xiii, xviii,
  35*n*; agricultural, 53–54, 64, 65–66;
  cost of, 56, 68, 70*n*, 85–86; explanation of 80 percent estimate, 83–85;
  from lake and ocean floors, 56, 59*n*;
  from organic wastes, 55, 64; from
  sewage systems, 54–55
Resources, defined, xii, xiv, xv
Rice, conversion to calories, 43*n*
Rich, C. I., 113*n*
Robertson, L. S., 43*n*
Rohlich, G. A., 112*n*
Running out. *See* Exhaustion of phosphorus
Runoff, phosphorus loss from, 41–42,
  53

Sauchelli, Vincent, 45*n*, 57*n*, 59*n*, 110,
  113*n*
Sea water, phosphorus in, 19
Seay, Edmond E., Jr., 109, 112*n*

Sedimentary rock, phosphorus concentration in, 2
Sewage systems, phosphorus from, 54–55, 58n
Sheldon, Richard, 15, 18, 23n, 24n
Smith, Frederick E., 33n
Smith, George E., 45n, 112n
Soil: conservation, 107–08, 109–10; effect on crop output, 37; fixation of phosphorus in, 110–11
Soil erosion, 35n; control measures for, 108; cost of reducing, 108–10; phosphorus loss from, 41–42, 43, 53, 107–08
Sorghum, conversion to calories, 43n
South Korea, fertilizer usage, 98–99
Stanford, G., 112n
Strip mining, 8
Subeconomic deposits, xiv, xv, 4, 6
Supply of phosphorus. See Phosphorus reserves

Taiwan: fertilizer usage, 98–99, 105; multicropping in, 36
Taylor, A. W., 112n
Taylor, Theodore B., 49, 50, 57n

Technology: cost of phosphorus extraction and, 18, 24n; in crop production, 48–49
Terman, Gilbert L., 113n
TIE. See Institute of Ecology
Thorium, 7, 23n
2.7 power rule. See Power rule, 2.7

Uranium, 7, 23n
United Arab Republic, fertilizer usage, 98–99, 105

Waste discharge, from phosphorus: cost of, 8; disposal of, 9; in Florida, 21n; recycling, 54–55, 64
Weather, effect on crop output, 37
Weinberg, A. M., 7
Weinberger, Leon W., 55, 58n
Williams, Moyle S., 27, 34n, 37, 43n
Willrich, Ted L., 45n, 112n
Wind erosion, 112n

Yield-value index, 27–28, 31

Library of Congress Cataloging in Publication Data

Wells, Frederick J.
    The long-run availability of phosphorus.

    Bibliography: p.
    1. Phosphates. 2. Phosphorus. I. Title.
TN913.W44   333.8′5   74-6842
ISBN 0-8018-1656-4